Fore
For
Golfing Pleasure

Chris Land

Wellesbourne-Wormald

Published by Wellesbourne-Wormald
10 Charlotte Close
Mount Hawke
Truro
Cornwall
TR4 8TS

Cover Illustration by Arthur Pickering, East Looe, Cornwall
Typeset by Elaine Beckton, Truro, Cornwall.
This book production has been managed by Elaine Beckton.
Printed and bound by Pryntya, Redruth, Cornwall

By the same author:
North South & Overseas
an autobiography published
August 2000 – £10·95

Contents

Acknowledgement

My sincere thanks to my wife Gill, for the many hours spent checking the manuscript and correcting my appalling spelling.

Foreword

I have spent virtually my whole life around golf clubs and I have listened for many hours to some wonderful golfing stories, most of which are now lost in the mists of time. It is, therefore, highly unusual to find somebody like Chris Land who has committed his various recollections to print. This super book with its amusing, whimsical and poignant reminiscences will prove enjoyable to both established golfers, who will doubtless wander off down their own memory lane, and newcomers to this wonderful game as they realise just what pleasure a lifetime in golf can provide.

Gary Alliss

Professional
Trevose Golf and Country Club, Cornwall
April 2003

Introduction

CHRIS LAND was born on the 14th December 1936 near the village of Aldmondbury, south of Huddersfield, West Yorkshire. When he was ten he moved with parents and sister to a large manor house in Northam, North Devon, which his parents turned into a successful guesthouse. Following agricultural college and two years National Service in the Royal Artillery, he started his wanderings.

Firstly Tanganyika (now Tanzania), India, back to England, then Rhodesia and South Africa. He returned to live permanently in Cornwall in April 1992. Chris and his wife Gill are members of that fine links course at Perranporth. He has been playing this wonderful game of golf for 48 years.

Chapter One
How it all Started

'**F**ore,' shouted Richard Davidson.

I was at the top of my back swing at the 5th at Ceres, a lovely tree lined course in the mountains north of Cape Town. Why was he yelling fore before I had even completed the shot I wondered? A troupe of baboons were ambling across the fairway perhaps 150 yards ahead. 'You bloody fool Richard,' I said when we saw what he was shouting at. But we all loved it – what a wit – what a wonderful game!

I said to Boet Wessels, a retired university lecturer, 'There are very few shits who play golf.'

He replied, 'Yes, but its amazing how many bloody fools, idiots, monkeys, apes, baboons, silly asses, poopols (Afrikaans for fundamental orifice), tits, nincompoops, f...ing idiots, cretins, stupid bastards and village idiots play the game.'

I was surprised even startled that this rather dour, typically Afrikaner member of my four ball at Margate Country Club on the Natal South Coast, South Africa, should make such derogatory remarks about fellow golfers. I looked at him again and saw that he was smiling at me through his thick pebble glasses. 'Come Chris man,' he said, 'this is what golfers call themselves in sheer frustration after making a nonsense of a shot,' and he laughed at my naïvety. Of course he was right, but I'd never thought of it that way before. Usually the worse the golfer, the worse the curses.

Forty-seven years of golfing pleasure to date started for me at the age of eighteen on the beach at Westward Ho! The old man had kept saying, 'Why don't you give it a go lad!' in his pronounced Yorkshire accent, as broad as ever, despite eight years in North Devon. We were both Sagittarians and both of us loved sport. Up to then it had been rugby, cricket, tennis, athletics, beach hockey, even bowls. 'OK,' I said, and the old man gave me a couple of hickory-shafted irons and some balls and I proceeded to thrash them up and down the beach when the tide was out. Father started when he was forty and was then hooked for life. He'd play every day if he could and did so in retirement, well into his eighties.

Father was a member of Royal North Devon Golf Club, which abuts the beach at Westward Ho!, and so shortly after my beach initiation was I. His first club was called Longley, in a suburb of Huddersfield – then after the war, he bought a mansion with five acres of grounds in Northam, North Devon called Wellesbourne. He turned the property into a successful guesthouse, being a most practical man, with boundless energy and enthusiasm. It changed our lives; my parents, but more particularly my sister Linda's and mine.

General Hutchinson had had Wellesbourne built in the mid-eighteen hundreds and he and his son Horace – the first golfing scribe, as we now know them – were founder members of Westward Ho!, in 1864, the oldest golf course in unbroken use in England. Horace was also a fine golfer and on winning one of the first monthly medals at the tender age of sixteen, automatically became Club Captain for the next twelve months. The recently constituted rules had to be changed rather quickly; one couldn't have a sixteen-year-old boy as Club Captain.

A young village boy, a caddie at the club, was boot boy at Wellesbourne. His name was John Henry Taylor. He soon became a fine golfer, turned professional and won 'The Open Championship' on more than one occasion around the year 1900 and was one of the famous triumvirate (the others were Harry Vardon and James Braid), who carried all before them in those days. It was a touching gesture by RND that JH, as he was universally known, was elected President of the club in 1957.

★★★

'Come in,' in a peremptory, stentorian voice, was how Stanley Taggart described to me the reply to his nervous knock on the secretary's door. It was his first interview as a rather timid young north country professional with the then RND secretary.

Major Andy Garland, a retired Assam tea planter, was sat bolt upright behind an enormous polished desk with nothing on it but inkwells and that day's copy of 'The Times', Stanley said.

'Ah, you must be Taggart,' the Major barked, 'sit down and tell me about yourself young man.'

Stanley sat down, cap in hand, and half an hour later was delighted to be confirmed the new professional. For the first ten years at the club he wasn't permitted to use the clubhouse; then he was made an honorary member and became a well-liked friend to all, especially to us younger chaps. Finally after retirement as club professional, the ultimate accolade, he was made Club President for a year. 'Taggart,' had certainly come the full circle.

When my father joined RND in 1947 membership was strictly limited to the local gentry and professional people like solicitors, doctors, Church of England vicars and officers in the armed forces. Those in trade, such as shopkeepers, artisans and manual workers, had no option but to join the 'Artisans Club' if they wanted to play golf. Artisan members were barred from the clubhouse, played at odd times – usually from first light – so as not to conflict with the members and changed in a ramshackle tin shed behind the pro's shop. But it all changed in the sixties. Artisans were allowed to apply for full membership and many of them soon became influential members of the club and served their terms as Captain, Chairman and President. The 'winds of change' were blowing through elitist Westward Ho! just as it was through many other eminent clubs countrywide.

The old man came out of the war with the rank of Lieutenant Colonel and was proposed for membership by Colonel Portman, a local squire, who had been in the same mess as father during the war. It was hard for him for many years, for his north country accent did not exactly fit, but he was a good man and well-liked and he eventually made It.

Westward Ho!, or Royal North Devon as it became known after acquiring its prestigious royal patronage, is a true 'links' course immediately behind the pebble ridge. This massive barrier of pebbles, reputed to have been washed across from Hartland Point in the west by winter storms, effectively stops the sea from swamping the course. But the course is on common land and friction between commoners and club members has been an ongoing problem ever since.

From ancient times if you owned a hearth in the nearby parishes of Northam, Appledore or Westward Ho! you were entitled to run small stock on the course – which was part of Northam Burrows – free of charge. Stock being geese, sheep and goats and a cow or a horse – provided the horse was unshod. Hearth owners were known by the quaint name of 'potwallopers' and for this privilege were expected to assemble with their families on the burrows on Easter Monday each year, to throw back the pebbles onto the pebble ridge, which had been washed off by winter storms. A fine spread and copious liquid refreshments were supplied by the Lords of the manor and a good time was had by all. However from the founding of the golf course in 1864, animosity gradually built up between the golfers and the potwallopers. In those early feudal times the golfers rode roughshod over the potwallopers (some of whom were artisan members) and in those days there was little the potwallopers could do about it. But by the second half of the last century with the advent of the emancipation of the working man, the potwallopers started getting their own back.

Sheep doubled and trebled in numbers and a riding school put out up to a hundred horses, mostly illegally shod. Consequently every blade of grass was devoured as it came through and the horses in particular were soon close to starvation. Erosion inevitably followed and sand from the sand hills, which were denuded of marram grass, eaten in their desperation by the horses, blew onto part of the course and choked it.

One of the many rules and regulations drawn up to regulate the use of the burrows, was that the golf club was only permitted to fence off a third of the eighteen greens at any one time. So the sheep and even sometimes the semi starved horses would nibble bare patches of grass on the unfenced greens. Desperately disheartening to the green-keepers and golfers alike. At the height of the impasse, some greens were even vandalised – chunks were dug out of them and some were damaged by waste oil and chemicals.

But the paramount daily disaster was the herd of horses galloping full pelt across the course to the rubbish dump. The local council decided in the fifties to establish a groyne – rather like a pier – to ensure that the water from the Torridge estuary didn't encroach onto the eastern end of the burrows, when particularly high spring tides occurred. This mile long groyne was constructed over a twenty-year period, by the dumping of household refuse. When the dustcarts trundled up in the mornings to dump their loads of rubbish the famished horses, wherever they were on the course, pricked up their ears and then headed full tilt for the dump. For of course the refuse contained pieces of bread and other edibles, which the horses ravenously consumed. The mad gallop was of course in the nearest straight line from where each horse was to the dump, and if a few unprotected greens, or unwary golfers were in the way, so be it. It was heartbreaking for the green-keepers and the concerned golfers, but the horse owners were only getting what they felt was their own back. Years of suppression, by what they saw as high-handed toffs who now were getting their pay back.

At last, I am told, common sense and mutual understanding has become the order of the day – not before its time.

Chapter Two
Westward Ho!

The resort of Westward Ho!, is a mecca of the traditional British holiday by the sea. Golden sands stretch for miles until the estuary of the two rivers, Taw and Torridge, meet the sea. Before the car holidaymakers arrived at Bideford by train then onward to Westward Ho!, in horse drawn carriages. With the advent of the motorcar, the seaside village itself soon became very crowded, so visitors naturally spread out. The inland lake behind the pebble ridge became very popular and to get to it, it was necessary to cross the golf course by car. By the nineteen-sixties, at the height of the holiday season in August, cars were crossing the course in both directions, virtually nose to tail. This rough road runs parallel to the 18th and 2nd fairways, but bisects the 17th and 3rd fairways. Without a marshall the drive at the 3rd and the third shot into the par five 17th, was one long exasperating wait.

Jimmy Heywood said to us, 'I'm going to go, I'm sure I can clear the road,' So he hit his shot to the 17th green and it landed full toss on the roof of a car. 'We've got problems now Jimmy. Why the hell didn't you wait?' somebody said. The car screeched to a halt and a man got out and walked all round it, then got on his hands and knees and looked underneath. He then looked up into the sky, shook his head totally mystified then got back into his car and drove off. He never thought to look up the 17th fairway, where four golfers were trying to hide behind each other and at the same time holding their sides in stitches of laughter.

It was the late dear old Jimmy (who was tragically killed in Malaya by an articulated lorry) who asked me to attend the flag during a medal round together. 'You are an idiot Chris,' he said with his slight stutter. I pulled out the flag and out came flag and cup together and of course the ball struck the cup. Penalty. Ah well, I did try!

Easter Monday 1965, the important Easter meeting. It had poured down throughout the round and the gale force southwesterly, soaked and froze us. Tony Waldeck (my first brother in law) and I were longing for the sanctuary of the clubhouse and had long since given up trying. 'What do you think I should take now?' Geoff Thornton said to his caddie. Geoff was probably twenty years older than us and well able to afford a caddie. We were halfway down the 17th fairway, he had had around 107 blows already and, deadly serious, he was asking his caddie this fatuous question. Oh, wonderful eccentric Englishmen! Tony and I sat down on the partially flooded fairway and burst into hysterical, uncontrollable laughter. That tale was told and retold over the years and it became a Westward Ho! legend.

Stanley Taggart told us another classic almost in the same league. Every Saturday afternoon Stanley as resident professional was hired for a round by a wealthy solicitor member. Stanley said, 'We had just driven off the 3rd – it was the height of the holiday season – when we saw two fellows sitting in the double pot bunker in their vests and shorts drinking beer out of a bottle.'

'Do you realise you are on a golf course and sitting in a bunker?' said the solicitor, marching up to the bunker and admonishing them in his rather pompous way.

The larger of the two men, who had a beer belly on him to be proud of, had of all things a trumpet with him. He staggered rather uncertainly to his feet saying not a word, but blew a loud blast on the trumpet in the solicitor's face and then collapsed back into the bunker again. The solicitor was nonplussed and Stanley said he almost drew blood in biting his lips, whilst desperately trying to keep his composure.

The bunkers were also regularly used for tea parties and procreating future generations.

One fabulously wealthy client of Stanley's was Philip Scrutton, the Walker Cup golfer. He would pitch up from time to time in his Aston Martin having driven down from Liverpool, where he had inherited the family stevedore business. He would say, 'Come on Stanley, let's have a round together,' and off they would go. He loved Westward Ho! On one visit Stanley said he had forgotten to bring his clubs. 'Sell me a set, Stanley,' he said. So he bought a set, wrote out a cheque on the spot, went round in the low seventies with them, left them with Stanley and forgot to pick them up. 'He never did pick them up,' said Stanley shaking his head.

I have never had a hole in one and only saw my first playing with my good friend Ren Jupp, who aced the 16th at Perranporth. In 1965 I saw my first – or thought I did – at the 8th at Westward Ho!

A pleasant grey-haired old boy asked to join us. He said he was from Surrey. So he and I took on Tony Waldeck and David Pennington. 'You won't believe it, but I've been playing for the best part of forty years and have never had an ace,' he told us. 'It would make my day,' he mused almost to himself. He took a seven iron when we reached the 8th and hit a beauty straight at the flag and in it went. 'I've done it, I've done it at last,' and he capered around, shook us all by the hand and off he went ahead of us at a fast trot to the green. Westward Ho! flags in those days, had a whipping of steel wound round the bottom of the pin to reinforce them against the depredations of the often gale force winds on the exposed course. The ball was hidden from view, one inch behind the hole and it wasn't his first hole in one after all. The poor chap was inconsolable, but what could we say; we felt desperately sorry for him.

Perhaps the main, almost unique feature of Westward Ho! is the giant sea rushes. They flood the centre of the course and their menacing presence petrifies all but the most intrepid single figure golfer. You have to drive over them to reach most fairways and if you hook or slice you are in them again. If, for example, you are too timid at the 10th and go for the shortest carry, you are likely to end up in the rushes on the far side. The rushes are tightly packed together, with just the odd patch of closely sheep cropped grass in between. They stand almost four feet high and have vicious pointed and very painful spikes at the end. I once drove a spike into my thumb which festered and had to be removed by local anaesthetic three months later. Various itinerant elderly gentlemen patrolled the rushes with their dogs, and each had his own zealously guarded patch! You topped into the rushes, the dog burrowed into them and found your ball – the dog got a tit-bit, you paid up and you had your ball back, which would otherwise have been lost. But you always wondered – did the dog pick up the ball which perhaps hadn't gone into the rushes and was still playable?

'There is a little white haired old boy with a white Scottie, who always picks up your ball whether you are in the rushes or not,' I said, after a few pints in the clubhouse following a Bideford RFC home game. 'The little sod annoys me intensely; the games hard enough as it is, without having to pay up for a ball which probably wasn't lost in the first place,' I continued, warming to my subject. 'You're talking about my father Christopher,' said one of our staunchest lady supporters. 'He wouldn't do a think like that, I know he wouldn't,' she said. What a predicament I had landed myself in. I spluttered and apologised – would I ever learn?

Jack Boyle's fourball, the brother of the owner of the prominent Bideford mens outfitters of that name, was holding our game up at every hole. By the 10th I could stand it no longer. 'Do you realise you have been holding us up all afternoon, you old fool,' I said. 'Why don't you let us through, don't you know the rules of golf?' I fumed. He turned red, stuttered and stammered, but couldn't get a coherent word out – so we just went through. I was perhaps twenty-eight at the time and he in his sixties. He died a few days later! I suppose I should have felt remorse, but I didn't. If you are holding the following match up you let them through; the very basic rules of golf, no matter who you are, or what age you are.

But perhaps the story of Westward Ho! I love above all others is that of the gallant Colonel and his increasing frustration with the game. It was in the very early days and may well have been apocryphal, but on reaching the 2nd green the Colonel grabbed his bag from his caddie, clambered over the pebble ridge and proceeded to wade as far as he could into the breakers. One by one he hurled the offending clubs as far as he could into the sea. 'There go and rest in hell,' he is reported to have said. 'I never want to see the damned things again,' he shouted to his caddie. When the tide went out, so the story goes, the caddie retrieved all the clubs and then sold them back to the Colonel the day after.

The course record of 65 by an amateur was set In the nineteen sixties and most probably still stands. But the unofficial record was one! Some intrepid hacker had apparently stood on the 1st tee and had unleashed an almighty slice-cum-shank, which flew off the club face and holed out on the nearby 18th green!

Chapter Three
Westward Ho! Again

My first job overseas, after leaving the army and National Service, was in the far-flung remotest part of Tanganyika, where I met some interesting characters, to say the least. Mike Hood-Cree and Roger Case – known as the 'hooded-crow' and the 'head case' respectively – turned up together with Mike's girlfriend at the Easter Meeting of 1964. The two of them were wild bachelor friends of mine in the bush.

Mike was well built with a mop of unruly wavy black hair and was given to gesticulating with both hands during general conversation. He laughed a lot and you saw the whites of his eyes and uniform gleaming white teeth when he did so. Roger was slimmer with fine mousey coloured hair which was always falling over his eyes and was repeatedly thrown back with a toss of his head. He had a weak chin and plummy accent to go with it and a happy smile with laughter lines around his eyes. I hadn't met Mike's girlfriend before – she was a tall striking girl with blond hair and a very assured way with her.

I walked into the packed bar at Westward Ho! which was full of animated conversation, when the two of them caught sight of me. 'Jambo Landy boy – Jambo, Jambo,' they both chorused (Jambo being 'greetings' in Swahili). We shook hands warmly and I joined them at the bar and was introduced to Carolyn. They hadn't changed much, they were still wild bush boys and so different from the assembled throng.

'It's good to see you guys,' I said a little apprehensively, for I could see more than one pair of eyes looking our way and saying to each other, 'Who are these strange friends of Chris Land's?' They had obviously had a few already, but another round was soon lined up. Then Mike brought out his pipe, lit it, drew deeply on it and then handed it to Carolyn. He then filled and lit another pipe and totally unconcerned, the two of them smoked and carried on talking to Roger and me, as though it was the most natural happening in the world. The room went strangely quiet, for it certainly gave the members a new topic of conversation that day.

Mixed hockey on the beach at Westward Ho! during school holidays was hugely popular. Often thirty or forty of us would turn up, the pitch was marked out on the sand and Captain Bocket-Pugh RN, the father of two of the girls, would invariably umpire. He had a shiny bald pate and a loud booming voice and didn't brook any nonsense. I always remember that one of my contemporaries, John Youngman, didn't bother to play hockey, but practised golf on his own for hours on end instead, which at the time seemed rather strange to us. He was a quiet somewhat reserved boy and we couldn't understand why he didn't join us on the beach.

All the practise worked however – he quickly got down to low single figures – went up to Oxford – got his blue and suddenly the world opened up for him. He married into money, his wife was also a good single figure golfer and in due course he became MD of his wife's family's internationally known manufacturing business.

Similarly at my agricultural college there was a young woman student by the name of Sophie Gestetner. Not by any stretch of the imagination could Sophie be described as even remotely beautiful or even attractive, but she was never short of an escort – they were like flies round a honey pot. The name Gestetner was enough!

Youngman brought the Oxford and Cambridge golf sides of that time down to Westward Ho! and many of these wealthy stylish young men joined the club as a result. All from being able to hit a golf ball. The old saying, 'It's not what you know, but who you know,' is so very true. For golf is one of the very few games that one can play well into old age and influential captains of industry and the like, are flattered to be seen playing with outstanding young golfers and often reward them with big career opportunities.

There is also an accepted convention in golf that no matter who you are, at the golf club you are addressed by your Christian name. The schoolboy, the plumber and the electrician, are Charles, Jim and Harry, the same as the General, the Admiral and the Barrister, are William, Ted and Hubert – quaint, but rather nice.

Another strange custom of fairly recent vintage, is the habit of golfers taking their hats off to each other at the end of a round; no doubt as a result of watching the pro's doing the same on TV. A gentleman will always remove his hat to salute a lady at the end of a mixed round, but not to a fellow male golfer. A firm handshake is the norm and quite sufficient.

There was 'Whisky Buck', and 'Old Buck.' Respectively the brothers were EH and TC Buckland. Whisky Buck was rarely seen on the golf course for he was expected to imbibe copious quantities of the fine amber liquid with his customers and as a result, his health was not as robust as his brother's. Old Buck was a portly gent, almost as wide as he was tall and he always wore tweeds, summer and winter, a pork-pie hat and thick pebble glasses. Whenever I was at home, between overseas tours, he would take the old man and me on and give us two bisque and invariably a beating. He was always straight down the middle and just long enough to clear the rushes, for he had been a low handicapper in his youth. On a cold winter's day he would take a spare ball out of his pocket usually on about the 6th tee. It had been nestling there next to a couple of warm jacket potatoes; for a warm ball flies much further than a cold one. He knew all the tricks, did Old Buck. His favourite quip when we had all missed the green at a short hole was turning to me, and engaging me with his twinkling eyes, he would say 'Land, tell me – which would you prefer; a virgin green or a green virgin?' and then followed by a deep prolonged guffaw, 'Ha, ha, ha!' It amused him no end.

Then there was dear old Stalybrass – he stuttered badly and couldn't get his C's out. One day he was trying to introduce my father – who was known formally as Colonel Land. After half a dozen unsuccessful attempts at, 'Let me introduce you to Cu-cu-cu-' he turned to my father and said, 'For Christ's sake, tell him your name.' The old man loved re-telling that one.

In 1964 we had our Centenary celebrations and all the 'who's who' of golf were invited, for it was the first golf centenary in England. A fourball challenge match was arranged between four top professionals of the time. Peter Allis and Brian Huggett played Christy O'Connor and Max Faulkner; with Christy and Max regaled in the attire of 1864 and using clubs and balls of that era. They dressed in plus-fours and Norfolk jackets, deer stalkers, waistcoat and tie and played with hickory shafted clubs and gutta-percha balls. Peter and Brian wore conventional clothes and played with the clubs and balls of 1964 and of course they gave a generous number of shots. Christy drove the fearsome 4th bunker – a towering monster even today – to wild acclaim from the motley crowd of followers, and capped a fine exhibition by knocking a mashie over the burn at the 18th, one bounce straight into the hole for a birdie three.

'What do you think of that then?' he said in his broad Irish brogue once the tumultuous applause had died away. 'It takes an Irishman to show you English how to play the game,' he said to Peter Allis. We all loved it.

There was a grand banquet and cocktail parties and towards the end of one such, when many were beginning to drift away, I met Henry Longhurst. We drank together – he double G&T's and me beer. I was actually chatting to the famous Henry Longhurst, a high point to remember and cherish. The morning after he was already ensconced in the bar and I went up to him and said, 'Hello Henry, how do you feel after our session last night?' He looked at me blankly. He obviously didn't know who the hell I was!

Chapter Four

The Two Davids

There were two David's in my regular fourball in the late fifties and sixties – as disparate a pair you couldn't wish to meet. The younger of the two, David Pennington, was about three years younger than me. A talented golfer good enough to get down to 4 handicap; he was afflicted by violent mood swings, from a beatific grin through thick glasses when all was going well, to the depths of moody depression and club throwing, when the ball didn't do his bidding. Swashbuckling David Lloyd–Davies on the other hand, had an impish grin always playing on his smiling face, perhaps twenty years older, he was an equally good golfer and took great delight in gently baiting Pennington, whenever the latter was having a hard time. Stanley Taggart, whenever he could get away from his duties as club professional was often the third member and I made up the fourball, a very average 8 handicapper at best. If Stanley couldn't play, Ken Whitfield usually filled in. Ken was player manager of Bideford Football Club, a centre half in his heyday with Manchester City and Wolves. He arrived in Devon with an 8 handicap and being a natural sportsman, with time on his hands during the week, soon got down to scratch.

Saunton was one of our favourite battlegrounds as Lloyd-Davies was an Ear, Nose and Throat specialist at nearby Barnstaple Infirmary. He would arrive in his Bentley in a dark three-piece suit and would be changed and ready for action shortly afterwards. We also played throughout Devon, especially in 'Open' tournaments.

Tom Pennington, David's father owned the New Inn Hotel in Bideford, a much-frequented hostelry by visiting golfers and the bar by locals alike. So David from a very early age became steeped in golfing lore. If you wanted to yarn about golf, you went to the New Inn and invariably found kindred spirits to while away a happy hour or two. On one occasion in my haste, I forgot to remove my badge – I was 'Sporty' at a local NALGO holiday camp. 'Sporty,' Tom Pennington greeted me. 'Come and meet Sporty chaps,' said Tom, his protruding belly wobbling with glee and his eyes twinkling with laughter. It was a long time before I lived that one down!

David was of medium height, slim with a good head of brown hair and grey eyes that sparkled behind his ever-present glasses, when he was in good humour. When he wasn't his face would turn a deathly white and a hurt expression would cross his features and his glasses would steam up. Westcountry drizzle on the golf course was a regular frustration. 'It's all right for you,' he would say. 'You try wearing glasses in this stuff. I might just as well walk in,' he would mumble and mutter to himself. David was an educated man, but he affected a slight Devonshire drawl – no doubt so that he appeared in the hotel, all things to all men. His pride and joy was his Triumph TR2. 'I'm going to push it past a hundred,' he said one day, when we reached the Braunton dual carriageway on the way to Saunton golf club. 'We've done it,' he shouted his face glowing with excitement, 'It's the first time past 100.' It could so easily have been the last time too, for every moving part of the vehicle was rattling ominously and the end of the dual carriageway had arrived with startling rapidity. But as far as he was concerned he had made the much-coveted three figures and he was totally elated.

The other David was a happy-go-lucky Welshman, always in good humour and always with a happy smile on his frank open face. His stocky frame, around 5'9" tall, was ideal for golf and he certainly gave the ball an almighty wallop, talking and cracking jokes all the time. He didn't conform and his fellow medical practitioners and some of the club members who thought themselves part of the local hierarchy, tended to look down on him. But he didn't give a damn and cheerfully laughed in their faces. 'They can go and get stuffed for all I care,' he would say. 'Pompous asses,' followed by a roar of profane laughter.

Stanley the pro was a Lancastrian from Bolton, with an accent to match. He was a bit of a Brylcream boy; slim, neat and swarthily handsome, with a pencil thin moustache and an eye for the ladies. He told us that he won the Italian Open at the age of eighteen, then the war came and when it was over, he never quite reached the same heights again. He loved to be considered 'one of the boys' and preferred our company when not on duty, to that of some of the more staid club members. His classic, which he regularly told to whoever would listen, was playing in a mixed foursome in the Manchester Alliance, 'Aye,' he would say, 'I knocked it on on a short hole for one and she knocked it off for two,' and he would laugh and shake his head in amused recollection. Sadly, now in his mid-eighties, I'm told he's gone downhill rather fast. One never knows what awaits one!

When Ken Whitfield joined us, his main contribution to the day, was his excellent golf. He had such a broad Geordie accent that any comments he made went unanswered, for none of us could understand him.

We had to let the fourball behind us through one day, at the 13th hole at Saunton. 'Odd place to loose a ball,' said one of them as he thanked us, 'must have been one hell of a smother to reach those rushes.' We were searching for David Pennington's driver, not his ball. A bad drive and the club went flying in a fit of temper and now to his embarrassment we couldn't find it. But relief was at hand. 'What about this,' said David Lloyd-Davies, sporting the broadest of broad grins. He had found an old child's potty in the rushes and now came forward to present it on one knee to Pennington. Even 'Penners' had to laugh, for we were all in stitches.

For once David Pennington and I, playing as partners at Churston in South Devon were going great guns. I was having one of my better days and David's face was a picture of happiness. 'Stop!' commanded Lloyd-Davies. I was at the top of my backswing on the 10th tee, when unbelievably, slowly and sedately, along the road in front of the tee, came a funeral cortegè. We all stopped and took off our caps and stood respectfully at attention until the cortegè had passed. 'You bastard, Lloyd-Davies,' cried Penners. For when I played the shot again I had a complete duff – I also had a shot at that hole – and the impetus was gone. 'That was pure gamesmanship, there was plenty of time to let him finish his shot,' Penners fumed. Lloyd-Davies just smirked and he and Stanley went on to win the match.

David Pennington and I always played in the Bideford Bay Foursomes together; eighteen holes at Saunton, then the day after eighteen holes at Westward Ho! Even in those days it was a big competition, now it has almost countrywide status. The build up to the eagerly awaited event held in April each year, consisted of many pints and many hours of animated discussion at the golf club or the New Inn. By the time the starter called our names, we were invariably in a state of high tension and excitement.

I always drove off the first tee. At Saunton a large patch of brambles, fifty yards in front of the tee, often attracted my ball and at Westward Ho! the adjacent burn, was usually the beneficiary. David was never amused and the atmosphere between us was severely constrained until things started to improve. One year we actually came in second, mainly I think because our opponents were a couple of miserable old devils and this really made us concentrate.

One year David killed a rook at the second. There was a flock of them probing the turf, probably for leather jackets and obscured from the tee by a low range of hills. His drive was long, low and hooked. The birds heard the ball coming, rose into the air as one, but one was struck by the ball and killed outright. David of course was furious that he had lost perhaps 100 yards of distance. 'Those bloody rooks,' he said, white with anger. 'Poor devil,' I replied. 'What do you mean, poor devil, that may cost us the tournament,' he retorted shaking his head in angry frustration. But that was David.

Bob Redfern was Devon County Champion in the mid-sixties. He was a very tall slim young man with receding swept back, fair hair, a shy attractive grin and according to Stanley Taggart a wonderful pair of hands for golf. I worked for the Potato Marketing Board at the time and he for the Egg Marketing Board. A friend of Bob's, Roger Luxton from Exeter, had a party piece when we were all together which he never tired of. He would introduce us and say, 'Egg meet Spud,' and promptly fall about in a paroxysm of laughter. He, if no one else, certainly got a lot of pleasure out of it.

The occasion I always remember Bob by was a County meeting at Teignmouth. The course is close to, but high above, the sea and consequently is often blanketed by fog. Each pairing disappeared out of sight into the pea-souper and the starter gave them a few minutes to get out of range, before announcing the next lot. 'Mr Redfern, County champion, on the tee please,' said the starter. Bob teed this ball up and unleashed one of his high drawn specials into the fog. A few seconds later came back a plaintive disembodied 'Oi!' He had hit a big one through the pair in front. 'Sorry Mr Starter,' said Bob and proceeded upon his way, midst much hilarity.

In my youth I couldn't hit my hat, but I made up for it by being, although I say it myself, an excellent chipper and putter. I am over 6' tall and was pretty strong in those days, but I had what is known as a fisherman's flick or flying elbow, at the top of my backswing; in that it went back, flicked out sideways and then came down cutting across the ball, causing an almighty slice, with resultant marked loss in length.

One day in my mid-thirties whilst living in Rhodesia, having nothing better to do, I started experimenting. I managed to stop doing the 'fisherman's flick,' and started striking the ball the proverbial mile. I hadn't a clue where it was going, but it felt marvellous and as the years went by, I started getting some control without losing length. Then I had my first shank and my erstwhile brilliant chipping and putting disintegrated and I have never been able to get it back.

So it was that Penners and I stood on the 16th tee at Westward Ho! all square, against Stanley Taggart and the dreaded Lloyd-Davies. Penners selected his club and shielding it showed it to me, so that the other two couldn't see it. There was a blustering wind full in our faces, so I decided if he was talking a six iron, I would take a four iron, being so much shorter than him. I struck it well and the ball soared fully forty yards over the back of the green. The six iron I thought he had shown me was in fact a nine iron – I wasn't allowed to forget that one for a long time.

Around this time Penners suggested we go down and have a game at St Enedoc in Cornwall – he had played it once and said it was a super course. 'I'll borrow the old man's car,' he said. It was summer, 'We can leave after lunch and there should be no problem driving back after. It isn't dark until after ten.' 'OK! that sounds fine,' I replied, 'but I want to bring Carole.' She was my fiancée and wedding bells were due to ring in the not too distant future. 'If you must,' he said with his usual lack of enthusiasm for any distraction from the golf.

It was a glorious sunny day and we chatted away animatedly on the way down and soon we were taking on that very good links course. Halfway round David threw a tantrum; clubs and four letter words were flying in all directions! Then for the first time in our long golfing relationship I saw red. 'How dare you use that sort of language in front of Carole, you moron,' I shouted at him. 'Apologise David, or I will never play with you again.' He went very white and retorted equally angrily, 'That's it, if you are going to treat me like that Chris Land, we'll pack up now and go home.' 'Right,' I replied, 'let's go.' We drove back to Bideford. I spoke to Carole, but not a word was exchanged between David and me, nor did we speak to each other for fully six months after. Only then were we on speaking terms again and the outburst forgotten.

We had some hilarious sessions after golf on the club fruit machine. Ten bob in the kitty – the machine was comparatively straight forward, compared to the modern intricate flashing monsters. There were usually David Pennington, Stanley, Geoff Day – an accountant with a lovely sense of fun and infectious laugh – the excitable solicitor, Jeremy Wright and myself. Three red arrows paid out a sizeable sum, three cucumbers took the jackpot and the coins came thumping out to wild shouts of glee and much back slapping. But more often when the kitty was finished one of us would say, 'Another five bob and we'll go,' and then, 'half a crown for the road and we'll call it a day.' We mostly lost, but what fun we had.

'Hole in one,' the cry came welling out of thirty throats on the first tee at Moretonhampstead, followed by hoots of laughter. 'Is it your first, Jack?' someone said. Yet more laughter and more leg pulling.

The Manor House Hotel, Moretonhampstead, is on the eastern edge of Dartmoor. The imposing granite mansion was built for British Rail early last century and attached to it is a golf course. A crystal clear stream meanders through it and in May the rhododendrons, which line the fairways, are in magnificent full blossom.

My father – Jack Land – was teeing off from the elevated first tee in an Alliance meeting with Stanley Taggart the Westward Ho! pro. One wall of the Manor House was behind the tee and at right angles to it was the pro's shop, both linked by a sunken concrete pathway. Father was not much more than 5'8" tall and with my mother even shorter, how I became a strapping 6'1" is hard to fathom. He was slim and well muscled, sported a military moustache and a few long strands of brown hair, were carefully combed to try and cover an almost bald pate.

The ball had flown off the point of his driver, in his haste to get the opening tee shot over with and struck the pro's shop almost at right angles to the intended line of flight. It first ricocheted back and hit the pathway wall, then across and hit the Manor House wall and finally slowly trickled along the pathway and down into an open drain behind the tee. Hence the cry 'Hole in One!' 'I felt as daft as a little shirt button,' he told my mother that night. One of his favourite turns of phrase when he had made a fool of himself. But he had made his fellow golfers day. He took up the game, he told me, when he was forty and soon became totally hooked on it. He would happily play everyday given the chance and on retirement did so well into his eighties. Whenever I was staying at home between overseas jobs in the early sixties, the daily routine was invariably the same. I would have a late night boozing at either the New Inn or the Ring O Bells (known as the Clangers), get up late, followed by a bit of gardening or log sawing, then the old man would say, 'Come on lad lets have lunch and a knock.' I often felt like screaming at him, 'Not bloody golf again.' For much as I love the game, I couldn't play day after day, like the old man could.

Freddie Meadows owned an amusement arcade and gift shop on the sea front at Westward Ho! He was very much ex RAF; not a hair out of place, a 'Clarke Gable' pencil thin moustache and he always wore a bow tie. He came originally from Birmingham. Freddie and my father were good friends and were drawn against each other one year in the 'Prince of Wales' knockout cup. On the sixth tee Freddie said, 'Have a piece of my rock, Jack,' and brought out of his golf bag a stick of rock of the type he sold in his gift shop. Before father could answer he broke the rock on the top of father's golf bag and gave him a chunk. 'Thanks Freddie, it tastes good,' said father. The ding-dong match continued and the next time the old man selected a club, he found small pieces of sticky rock stuck to his grip for the hot weather had quickly melted it. 'Gamesmanship,' cried my father. 'Not at all,' replied Freddie, 'I was only being friendly.' Freddie went on to win the match, but father had the tale to tell in the clubhouse after.

My parents usually took their holidays apart, for one of them had to stay and keep an eye on the guest house. One of my father's favourite haunts was an hotel at Barton-on-Sea, close to Bournemouth, which had its own golf course. He met a very decrepit old brigadier at the hotel on the first evening, who challenged father to a game the day after. They met on the first tee and the brigadier got down on his hands and knees to tee up his ball – he couldn't bend because of severe rheumatism in his knees – and said in a peremptory gruff voice, 'What's your handicap?' Father replied, 'Eight,' when it was really twelve, for he felt sorry for the old boy. 'Right,' the brigadier replied, 'I'm six, you get two shots.' He then proceeded to thrash father 7 & 6. What a salutary lesson he was given – that was the last time he ever falsified his handicap.

For many years father had a regular Tuesday morning game with Frank Dennis and Andy Garland –the irascible ex-secretary who first terrorised the youthful Stanley Taggart. When Andy got too old to play and finally retired, father and Frank continued the weekly routine and Andy would totter into the bar and meet them for a drink when they had finished. Frank Dennis was some fifteen years older than the old man and had retired to North Devon, to a lovely bungalow overlooking the River Torridge. His career had been in banking in the cut-throat world of the East End of London and now in retirement he wasn't short of a bob or two. As the years went by his eyesight began to fail caused by glaucoma, until it was only my father watching every shot he played, that he was able to continue. He was eternally grateful to my father and was always coming up with most generous gifts for my mother. It was a touching sight to see two old men enjoying the twilight of their lives together in golfing comradeship.

Chapter Five
National Service

My first wild thrashes on the beach at Westward Ho! occurred, I think, when I was about eighteen. If only I had started at twelve as so many youngsters do these days, I might have been a half decent golfer. But alas at the beginning, I played round after round with the old man and then when I had got every possible fault well grooved into my swing, he sent me to Stanley Taggart for lessons. Poor old Stanley looked at me and shook his head, 'We're going to have to start from scratch, I'm afraid, Chris,' he said. 'If only the Colonel had sent you to me from the start, it would have been so much easier,' he smiled ruefully. He did his best but couldn't stop the flying elbow and fisherman's flick. However I have managed to get down to eight handicap, in three separate decades since the fifties – which is not that bad!

I started two years compulsory National Service in the Army in September 1956, having been deferred to complete a two year diploma course at Agricultural College. I tried for a commission but failed, so I stayed on as a training instructor for the rest of my time. Others on the intake, who also failed, were posted to far-flung exotic countries and their departure provided the spark for me to want to travel in the future. The 'Gunners' training camp was at Park Hall, Oswestry, Shropshire; so Oswestry Golf Club became the centre of off duty entertainment, coupled equally with the nearby nurses home.

Harry Wheetman of Ryder Cup legend was the most famous local luminary. 'Harry could drive this green,' or, 'Harry used to reach this green with a drive and a wedge,' the members would tell us. 'Really!' we would say and endeavour to look suitably impressed, for at one time or another it would seem Harry had driven most of the greens on the course. For reflected glory is all about golf's much cherished folklore.

John Barber played off a good ten, a Scot – appropriately called George Scott – was four and Tony Millward and I were hackers off twenty-four handicaps. John was the proud owner of a vast number of tees – he once told me how he had acquired them. 'What colour was it?' he would ask whoever had just driven off. 'Red,' came the reply. He would then say, having picked the tee up, 'Oh, this is a yellow one' and put it in his pocket and another tee joined the ever-growing collection. I also have a large plastic bag full of tees, but collected I might add, mostly legitimately. 'Would you like to look at my tees?' I often ask friends at Perranporth, tongue in cheek. 'I had 1542 at the last count.' A cross-section reply would be, 'Not just at the moment if you don't mind Chris, perhaps next year,' and so the banter would continue.

John Barber was 6'2" tall, straight backed, broad powerful shoulders, dark hair and a smile which tended to curl out of the corner of his mouth. He spoke in short sharp sentences and in retrospect, thinking back, he was a bit of a know all. But he was also a very good darts player and at his height, he would stick his chest out and go for the twenties and usually get them. 'What about 301 up?' he would say to Albert, having first charged Albert's glass with another pint of bitter. Albert was as short as John was tall and because of this, always went for the triple nineteens. 'Thank-ee maister,' he would reply taking a deep pull on his newly acquired pint. 'I'll take ee on.'

Albert was the village roadsweeper at nearby Whittington and invariably had a dewdrop on the end of his nose, which often miraculously stayed there throughout the game – or it if dropped off – a new one quickly formed in its place. He nearly always lost, but provided he had a pint at hand, he was happy and he revelled in the attention we gave him.

Like so many Scotsmen, George Scott must have been born with a golf club in his hand, for he was a very accomplished golfer. He and John would partner either Tony or me. 'Will you be having a wee gamble, John?' George would ask and John would reply, 'But of course George, usual stakes?' 'Aye,' said George with a knowing twinkle in his eye. And so the battle lines were drawn. John wasn't short of a bob or two and against George he was the loser more often than not. And so two of the first years of my golfing saga happily passed by and in September 1958 'civi' life and my first job beckoned.

From September 1958 to early February 1959, I lived the 'life of Reilly.' Golf, rugby, beer, women – coupled most days – either with sawing logs or digging in our large vegetable garden. It was an idyllic life; in the pub, often up to midnight (for it was long before the breathalyser), staggering out of bed at around 10am, followed by digging or logging for a couple of hours, when the old man would inevitably say, 'Come on lad its time for lunch, then we will go and have a knock.' Day after day, golf and more golf. After the round usually a session on the fruit machine and then somebody would say, 'I'll give Chris a lift home.' After supper, borrow the old man's car and away to the New Inn or Ring O Bells. Halcyon days! On Saturdays I played for Bideford Chiefs. I knew all the rugby songs from College days, so my selection was automatic, especially for away fixtures at far-flung Falmouth, Launceston and Wiveliscombe. Colonel and Mrs Wood were regular supporters, especially for away matches, arriving in their splendid old Lanchester. The Colonel always wore tweeds with a pork pie hat and would bellow his approval from the touchline, whenever Bideford scored.

'Wonder who that dirty bugger was?' the old man said. 'I wonder,' I replied, as we walked past a discarded 'French letter,' leaving the third tee. It had been me. It was so easy to get disorientated in the car at night, following a few too many pints after rugby – Rosie had enjoyed it too!

But too soon it all came to an end. Sir Robert Stapledon Bart, Governor of the Bahamas, was home on leave and staying with his sister, Miss Mariel. I was invited for a sherry with them and despite having consumed four pints of bitter after a Bideford Chiefs home game – fool that I was – I somehow managed to stumble through the ordeal. A friend of Sir Robert's was a big wig in the Crown Agents and I was offered a position as Assistant Farm Manager on the 'Groundnut Scheme', in what was then Tanganyika (now Tanzania).

One rule the old man drilled into me from the beginning, was always try and buy the first round of drinks. Funnily enough he wasn't much of a drinker himself, rarely having more than a couple of halves. But he insisted, 'A gentleman always stands his round.' It's stood me in good stead over the years, but times have changed. Chaps are now playing golf who can't really afford to play and others hang back and will accept a drink with no real intention of reciprocating. Yet others will have a shower and make sure that they are last into the bar and then say to the barman, 'How many are in for me?' So about three years ago, when we had walked onto the 18th tee I said, 'I suggest I buy drinks with you partner,' and to the other two, 'the two of you buy drinks together, I'm only staying for two half pints in any case.' There has been many a raised eyebrow when I have broached the subject since then, especially from those known to be tight fisted and shy to stand their round. Although I can well afford it, I refuse to be a one-man philanthropic society.

Early February 1959 saw the start of my life's great overseas adventure. Nachingwea was in the Southern Province of Tanganyika and close to the border with Mozambique, a hundred miles inland from the Indian Ocean coast and close to three hundred miles by rough dirt road to Dar-es-Salaam, the capital city to the north. You could drive to Dar in the dry season – from April to September – which was the only time the mighty Rufiji river was navigable. Cars were loaded onto an ancient primitive pontoon and an equally ancient tugboat laboriously towed the pontoon to the opposite bank, then Dar was only a matter of an hour's drive away. With the arrival of the first rains in October, the wet season started and the river rapidly became a swollen impassable torrent. Then the only way out of Nach was by the weekly Dakota which flew in from Dar in the morning –via Lindi and Mtwara on the coast – and returned, after a brief stop, to the capital. For six months of the year there was only one way to reach civilisation and that was by air on the weekly plane, which for all but the very wealthy, was financially out of the question.

Nachingwea – or Nach, as it was colloquially known – was a settlement of perhaps eighty to a hundred whites and one of the three areas chosen after the war by the then British Government (Tanganyika being a British Protectorate), to grow groundnuts, to satisfy Britain's urgent need for vegetable oil and margarine.

The club was the focal point of Nach social life, with the central workshops, agricultural experimental station, two Indian owned shops (known as dukas) and private houses clustered around it. The 'main trace', was a dead straight twelve-mile long dirt road leading straight into the bush from Nach. At intervals along the trace, sixteen farms each of at least 2000 acres had been hacked out of the virgin bush to grow the groundnuts. I became manager of farm 16. Three quarters of the farm managers were married and the remainder were mainly young bachelors like myself. There were only two single women in the whole of the Southern Province, both were nurses and not surprisingly, both were regularly chatted up. 'Black Magic,' was frowned upon, so our only relief was self-gratification and endless boozy sessions at the club. Tuesdays, to stock up with food and collect any mail brought in by the plane and the weekend, were the main club days.

Nach club was a spacious colonial style building with a swimming pool and two hard tennis courts. It was shaded by blue flowering Jacarandas and magnificent flat-topped Flamboyants. On two sides of the club was the golf course and in the middle of the golf course the cricket pitch. There were six holes on the course, three times round for an eighteen-hole competition. The greens were called 'browns', consisting of sand mixed with waste sump oil and the hole, in the middle of each brown, was never changed. As each match reached the brown, one of the caddies would smooth the brown prior to putting, dragging a sack half full of sand around, on the end of a broom handle. The fairways were sparsely covered in course grass, green in the wet season and brown, almost bleached white, in the dry season. Each golfer always carried a club with him as he walked round the course, for when the cry 'nyoka' (Swahili for snake) was heard, he was equipped to defend himself if necessary. But usually the snake took off at full speed towards the safety of the thick bush surrounding the course, chased by screaming excited caddies. Monkeys were the other main hazard, for the little devils would drop from the trees, grab your ball and make off with it. The caddies consisted of a motley crowd of half-naked little black children, who laughed and cavorted amongst themselves, taking little notice of what the golfers were doing.

When the round was over they would all line up for their 'shillingi', chorus 'Asanti sana' (thank you very much), then run off laughing among themselves, to gamble their hard-earned shillingi away with each other.

The teeing grounds were six-foot squares of sun-baked mud, each standing two feet above the surrounding ground. It was impossible to stick a conventional tee peg into the bone hard ground, so each player owned an ingenious assortment of rubber piping to put the ball on, cut off to different lengths and tied together with string and a lump of lead on the end – the latter so that you didn't lose the tees after the shot was played.

Tuesday and Saturday afternoons were golf days and Sunday morning also, provided a cricket match wasn't in progress. Most of the golfers were self-taught, so balls would fly in all directions, followed by curses and profane roars of laughter. Always played in the right spirit, golf was well supported, particularly the 19th hole, after a hot afternoon under a blazing tropical sun.

'Were those your golf clubs coming aboard at Durban?' I asked. 'Yes, I thought I'd bring them along just in case,' replied Boet Uys. 'Well, I've got mine with me as well,' I said. 'So we can have a round together whenever we dock.' 'Great,' he replied, 'I can't wait.'

I had joined the 'Europa' of the Italian 'Lloyd Tristino' line, for three weeks local leave halfway through my three-year tour. The ship plied between Genoa and Cape Town, calling at every port on the way south and again on the return journey. I boarded at Dar, Boet and I had a round at East London, Port Elizabeth and Milnerton golf club near Cape Town, the latter course with its breath-taking full frontal views of majestic Table Mountain. Then we played the same courses on the return journey and his home course – Durban Country Club. Why is it that ladies aboard ship are more obliging than when on home territory? Perhaps it's the sea air and carefree life on a cruise. Whatever, I more than made up for my eighteen months forced abstention in Nachingwea.

Chapter Six
The Plains of Assam

Uhuru' (freedom), 'Uhuru na kasi' (freedom and work) were the ever more strident cries in the middle of 1961. There was a 'rumble in the jungle', the Africans wanted their freedom from what they saw as the colonial oppressor. The ex-primary school teacher, Julius Nyerere, was waiting in the wings to become President and the erstwhile happy go lucky, cheerful workers, became sullen and uncooperative overnight. It was time to leave and the 'winds of change' coincided fortuitously with the end of my three-year tour. My sister Linda – who had come out for a holiday with me for the last eighteen months – and I, sailed back to England from Dar, in the lap of luxury on a BI liner. First calling in at Mombasa then though the Red Sea, Suez Canal, the Mediterranean, Bay of Biscay and home.

Once again I easily fell back into the indolent way of life I had enjoyed three years previously together with regular trips to London for interviews. This time I rather fancied a shot at the East, perhaps tea or rubber planting. I worked out a sly, underhand method of making the most of my train journeys to London, by organising two or even three interviews in one day and collecting travelling expenses for each one of them. But one day, inevitably the bubble burst. Two offers of employment arrived by the same post. One was rubber planting in Malaya and the other tea planting in Assam. Impulsive as ever, I said to my mother, 'What do you think?' She read the letters through and said, 'You are always in such a hurry Chris,' and then said, 'Daddy's playing with Andy Garland as he always does on a Tuesday morning – he used to be a tea planter – why don't you go down to the club and have a chat with them?' 'Good idea, I'll go straight away,' I replied. When I got to the club I met the secretary, Charles Stephens, who said they were still out on the course, so I walked across the burn, which runs between the 1st and the 18th and the road to the beach and met them on the 15th green. I waited until they had finished putting. 'Morning Major,' I said, then to the old man, 'two job offers came in the post this morning, one rubber and one tea planting. What do you think Daddy?' 'Go for the tea, Christopher. You'll never regret it. We used to work in the gardens until lunch and then played sport every afternoon – golf, polo, cricket and tennis – it was a great life,' said Andy. So on Andy Garland's advice alone, I chose tea planting in Assam.

The SS Iberia sailed down the Thames from Tilbury Docks in January 1962, first class P&O to Bombay. Only the very best was good enough for employees of Jardine Henderson Ltd, a Rolls Royce name in tea. From Bombay to Calcutta across the white-hot plains of India, in a train that never seemed to travel faster than a crawl. Then after kitting out in tropical gear in Calcutta, a rickety old Dakota to Jorhat, centre of the Assam tea estates.

Andy Garland's advice proved wrong; he was recalling the leisurely life of a tea planter before the Second World War. I was on my bicycle each morning and overseeing the labour by 6am, then lunch and the relief of a two hour lie back in the humid heat of the day and back into the gardens until 6pm. On Saturdays we were generously allowed the concession of an early finish at 5pm, so that we could play a couple of sets of tennis before dark, followed by volunteer snooker and often, when well into our cups, a visit to 'Granny's' brothel at nearby Mariani village. Sunday was bliss – we had the whole day off work!

In Andy Garland's time the first rather pleasant task a young assistant had to undertake on arrival in Assam, was to choose his 'old woman.' That was to choose a young Indian girl to run his household and administer to all his needs and from then on, whatever her age, she was rather incongruously known as his 'old woman.'

But in my time, independent India no longer permitted their young girls to be defiled by Europeans and so the only outlet for a young bachelor to let off steam, was in the rather seedy back street brothels, like Granny's. Tanganyika all over again! If only I had contacted my friend Jimmy Heywood in Malaya, to get his viewpoint before making the decision. For in Malaya it was totally acceptable, he told me later, for a young bachelor to have an Indian, Malay or Chinese woman as his girlfriend. Coupled with this lack of female company, Assam was stinking hot – far hotter than the hottest day I ever encountered in Tanganyika – and the work in the tea gardens was routine and boringly repetitive. Fifteen months later I was back in England, a four-year contract broken with the blessing of Jardine Henderson Ltd and a return voyage in the same grand manner and similar style, with which I went out.

On arrival in Assam, I was asked by Ken Holmes the Senior Assistant on my plantation, 'Do you play rugby?' I thought this rather an odd question and replied, 'Yes I do. But surely you don't play rugby in this heat?' 'We do,' he said, 'and, moreover, the 'All India' annual rugby tournament is in Calcutta in September and if you make the side it's a great weeks kel (Hindi for party).' I made the team, but only just; it was difficult to become adjusted to playing rugby in a sauna bath. It proved certainly a week to be remembered and surprisingly for Assam, we actually got through three rounds – as we were a team more renowned for our drinking abilities rather than our rugby prowess. Four of us became most unpopular with the team captain, by playing a fourball at magnificent palm-tree-lined, Royal Calcutta, rather than taking part in the seven-a-side tournament, which followed the main event. I never played rugby again. Hanging up my boots at the comparatively early age of 26 and concentrating on golf was a very sound move, for I had picked up no major rugby injuries and have in consequence enjoyed golf all the more since.

We played golf on Sunday mornings on the 'madan' adjacent to the Jorhat planters club – a vast ugly mausoleum of a building. India is overrun with so many millions of goats and rather forlorn looking fat tailed sheep, that every edible blade of grass is hungrily devoured almost as soon as it comes up through the ground. Indeed zero grazing was the only way to successfully keep dairy cattle in that overcrowded country. Cows are permanently tethered in stalls and the Assamese owner would walk to the nearest tea garden every morning on his long spindly legs, his dhoti flapping around his bony knees. He would squat down on his haunches and laboriously cut the grass between the tea bushes by hand, using a small curved sickle and then stuff it into a sack, hump it onto his shoulders and take it back to his cows. Protected from the goats and sheep amongst the tea, is the only place grass gets a chance to grow.

So the grass on the madan, which was criss-crossed by dharas (dry river courses), was even more sparse than on the golf course at Nachingwea and of a variety unpalatable even to half starved goats and sheep. 'Brown's' were again the order of the day and kites, the scavengers of India, known countrywide as 'shite hawks,' were the major hazard. They would swoop down and pick up any unguarded ball in their beaks and carry it away to their nests. Thus each golfer had to employ two caddies; one to carry your golf bag and the other to ward off the shite hawks. As you reached each tee the smallest of the two caddies, known as the agra-wallah (or fore caddy) was told by the other to, 'jow' (go in Hindi). Off he would run on his matchstick thin legs, to guard your ball once you had driven, until you were ready to play your next shot. The agra-wallah would very quickly get to know how far each golfer could drive the ball and no amount of entreaty, wild arm waving or cursing, would make him run any further. Embarrassingly the little sods were usually right. After the stinking heat of a morning's golf, it would be three or four IPA's (Indian Pale Ales) in the club to slake the thirst, then invariably a curry lunch at some senior planter's house. When you first arrive in India, you can usually manage a couple of curries a week, but in a very short while, like all the other planters you have a curry for lunch every day. On arrival at the palatial home you are straight away proffered a 'pinky' (a double pink gin) called 'tea planters ruin,' and then shortly afterwards the curry arrives brought in by the 'burra sahib's' bearer and his assistants, all dressed in sparkling white from fez to toe.

There would always be three bowls of curry to choose from – hot, very hot and to all but the bravest, hardened old planter, a totally inedible bowl. In colour the hot bowl was a dark brown and the hottest almost black. There was a mystique of pure snobbery attached to eating curry – the hotter you could take it without flinching, the higher your standing. I never progressed beyond the hot and I found even the hot at times took some stomaching. The meat in the curry was nearly always goat, (the cow being sacred in India, was never slaughtered for its flesh) and it was quite delicious. Curry in India was served only with rice, dahl and warm chapatti, smeared with butter and always followed by a sickly sweet pudding.

Sunday in Jorhat usually ended with a long afternoon 'lie back,' merging into evening and a sore head the morning after.

Chapter Seven
Back to England

Where I had been sweltering in the plains of Assam, back in England the winter of 1963 had been the coldest since the winter of 1947; but however cold and snowbound it was elsewhere in the country, the golf course at Westward Ho! was always open.

As the local ditty goes, sung to the tune of 'Jingle Bells' –

> Down in Westward Ho!
> they don't get no snow
> They don't get no snow
> down in Westward Ho!

The P&O liner I had sailed on to India, had gone on from Bombay to Australia and there were mainly Australians returning from Europe on board. Phil Kendall had said to me, 'If you ever want to work in Australia Chris, all you have to do is drop me a line.' 'Thanks,' I had said, 'one never knows what the future holds.' Phil was a partner in a livestock auctioneering and estate agency business, in the quaintly named town of Wagga Wagga, New South Wales – it was just the sort of work I fancied. Australia at the time was looking for Brits to settle in the country and the carrot was a passage costing only £10 and a free return to UK after three years if you didn't like it. So for the princely sum of £10, you could become an Australian – I couldn't fill in the form fast enough.

Once my application was lodged, I took a job as 'Sporty' at a local holiday camp and then walked out a month later after a disagreement with the manageress. Then I worked for Johnny Potter on the remote rural fringes of Exmoor, he was an agricultural contractor – hay baling and combining corn. It was hard work and the hours were long and irregular, but I was young and strong in those days and the pay was good for labouring work. At the same time I was getting the odd game of golf and actually got to the final of the prestigious 'Prince of Wales' annual knockout cup. And thereby hangs a tale.

In the quarterfinals I had beaten Colonel RDD (Dickie) Birdwood of Horewood House near Bideford. He was a rather diffident, but charming old ex-career solider – we both tried our best to give it to the other – but I just scraped through on the 18th. Then in the semi-finals I beat Johnny Goodban, 'Mr Saunton' in so many ways, who was President, Secretary and general factotum and just about kept that club going on his own. A Cambridge blue in his day and still a good golfer, but by then well into his seventies, despite his guile and wealth of experience, youth just prevailed. So in the final I met John Phillips, the club Chairman, in his golfing prime and playing off a two handicap. I was as nervous as a kitten standing on the 1st tee and so a big slice followed, which easily cleared the burn, but then drifted into a lateral water ditch. John came over to watch me play the shot and said, 'You know of course Chris that you can't ground your club in a water hazard.' Of course I knew, but what a clever ploy, smacking of gamesmanship. I duffed the shot, lost the hole, then the match out in the country. It was all good experience, but I never did get my name on the 'Royal North Devon' honours board. Runner up in that competition was the nearest I got to it in thirty-five years as a member or overseas member.

In the sixties Saunton, although a fine golf course, was very much the junior partner to Westward Ho! Another eighteen-hole course has been added since and the clubhouse extended and vastly improved, so that it is now the venue for many a national competition. Then it was famous, or more correctly infamous, for a coterie of members who indulged in very heavy drinking after golf, but the advent of the breathalyser soon put an end to that sort of excessive indulgence. I had only been back at home for a couple of months, when I was offered the full time Secretaryship of Saunton. I didn't accept the offer and in hindsight, I'm very glad I didn't even if only as a stopgap. The Secretary of a golf club in those days was usually a sinecure for a retired Army officer or similar and in no way the long-term career opportunity it is now.

Around this time unemployed people like I had become and many a retired person, had to visit the labour exchange in Bideford – perhaps it was to sign on or collect the dole – I can't remember why. However it soon became the venue to fix up that day's game of golf. Old Captain Morgan RN would say, 'Land, you fixed up for this afternoon?' 'No, Sir,' I would reply and in short time he and I had a game arranged with two retired Army officers, who had also been in the queue.

I remember with some amusement the first time I joined the unemployment queue. I was asked by the young lady behind the counter,

'What was your last job?' 'I was a tea planter,' I replied. She then flipped page by page through her book and said to me, 'I'm sorry we don't seem to have any vacancies for tea planters at present.' I managed to keep a straight face and said, 'Right, I'll try again next week.'

Then in August an official letter arrived in the post, informing me that I had been accepted for emigration to Australia. In typical bureaucratic fashion it had taken them four months to make up their minds and in the meantime I had become rather accustomed to life back in England again, so I turned the offer down. Now in semi-retirement, I would just love to live in Australia and so unfortunately would many thousands of others. You now have to prove that you have got over £300,000 in capital, to have any hope of even retiring there.

I told Johnny Potter I was leaving him –telling him the white lie that I was emigrating to Australia – and straight away started looking for a permanent agricultural job in England. I got lots of first interviews, but always seemed to falter at the final interview. 'Why should we employ a man of 27, with four years unrelated experience overseas, when we can take on a young man straight out of agricultural college and mould him into our ways?' they would say. Why indeed!

Finally, gratefully, I accepted a job as an Assistant Area Supervisor with the Potato Marketing Board, at the princely salary of £550 per annum, under half my salary when I left India. For seven years I worked from a base in Exeter, but often helped out other area offices for substantial periods of time, where big potato surpluses occurred.

I always took my golf clubs with me, wherever I went and as ever they opened many a door to a young man on his own when seconded to an unfamiliar part of the country. 'Looking for a game?' asked Willie Whitelaw, then MP for the Carlisle constituency and destined to become Tory party chairman in Margaret Thatcher's government. 'Yes indeed, I'd love one,' I replied. 'Good that gives us a four,' he said. He was a very good golfer off about six handicap and he and his two fellow club members great company on the very fine Carlisle and Silloth course overlooking the Solway Firth.

On another weekend at a loose end – I was staying in rather unpretentious, depressing accommodation in Kings Lynn – I took myself off to Brancaster on the North Norfolk coast. It was a horrid day; pouring with rain and for a time I was alone in the clubhouse at that renowned links course. Then three fellows walked in and shortly after the rain relented. One of them walked over to where I was sitting reading a magazine. 'Would you like to join us?' he asked. 'We might even get a full round in now that the rain has stopped.' 'Yes, please,' I replied. They introduced themselves by their Christian names and one of them said, 'Right Chris, you play with Arthur against David and myself.' On the first hole Arthur nearly holed his second shot and we won it with an easy tap in birdie. Arthur, was Arthur Perowne the well-known Walker Cup golfer, who came from those parts. Sadly the rain started again in earnest after we had played only four holes and drenched to the skin we trooped back to the clubhouse. If only for four holes, what an experience it was to play with a current Walker Cup golfer.

During a six months stay in the outskirts of Nottingham, I joined Hollinwell, that fine heathland course and almost every Sunday morning, had a round with Tony Radley (an old college friend of mine) at Newark Golf Club; followed by a slap up roast beef lunch at Tony and wife Honor's, Kirklington farmhouse.

Whenever I got a long weekend off work, I would drive down to stay with my sister at Hook near Basingstoke and my girlfriend Carole – shortly to become my fiance, then wife – drove up from Exeter. Linda had married Tony Waldeck, another total golf fanatic, the previous year, and we spent most of those weekends playing golf at 'Dorcdom', but really 'Bordon' nearby. Carole would say, 'Oh no, not 'Boredom' again,' and she would troop around the course with us and complain bitterly, 'I'm bored to tears, bloody game!'

Tony's golf could best be described as flamboyant; he had an exaggerated flowing swing, which he regularly checked whenever he passed a mirror and played off a totally unrealistic seven handicap. He had gradually tied himself up in knots, as there was no waist or shoulder turn in his swing, so much so, that he could hardly get the ball off the ground. I could give him a stroke a hole at the time and he still couldn't give me a game. Then one day he went to John Jacobs, then 'the' golf guru in the country. One of John's assistants was trying to sort him out, 'What on earth has happened to that poor fellow,' called out John from the other end of the range and forthwith took over from his Assistant, for he said, 'I haven't seen anyone in such a state, for a very long time.' Even the great John Jacobs had considerable difficulty in sorting Tony out.

The RAF was Tony's career and one classic remark of his was, 'Fall out the officers, other ranks stand fast,' usually when someone had belched or farted at an inopportune moment. He made an equally amusing comment about a fellow from the Assam rugby team I had played in, who came for a brief visit to Wellesbourne, when Tony was also there, 'His breath would take a coat of paint off the sideboard,' he said.

Every year during the last two weeks of August was the eagerly awaited 'August Meeting' at Westward Ho! A large number of country members from all parts of England would come down with their families and join the locals for a golf jamboree, only to be missed for very exceptional pressing commitments. For many years the AGM was held at the conclusion of the August Meeting and thus effectively the country members shaped the running of the club rather than the locals. It took sometime for the locals to get this position reversed and the AGM scheduled for when the country members were not around.

The highlight of the second week of the meeting was the 'Schoolmasters Cup', a knockout competition with full handicap allowance. It started on the Saturday and the previous evening saw an auction of each player, with the dapper Freddie Meadows in trademark floral bow tie, the Master of Ceremonies. He always found something amusing to say about each golfer before auctioning them, which got the main week off to a flying start. One year whilst on holiday specifically to play in the meeting from South Africa, I was drawn in the first round against Brian Fulford on holiday for the same reason, from Brazil. The following Sunday was the Premier competition of the year, the Kashmir Cup, 36 holes of stroke play and then the following day the best of Westward Ho! would take on the Oxford and Cambridge Golfing Society.

Talking about the Kashmir Cup, reminds me of the two rather eccentric brothers – Willie and John Moberley – country members of long standing both, who always volunteered to go out at the head of the field in the Kashmir and thus set the pace for the day. They were both single figure golfers, would never each go round in more than eighty blows and most important of all rarely took more than two and a half hours for the round. Compare this to the monthly medals these days, where three and a half hours is considered fast and a four hour round usual and acceptable. Watching the pro's on the accursed TV with their elaborate preparations before actually playing the shot, has greatly influenced the average club golfer. He now thinks it is correct to always take at least one practise swing before playing the shot, whereas the old hand just gets up and hits it. But of course you can't tell them!

I was chatting to Stanley Taggart near the first tee on Kashmir Cup day when he said, 'Do you see that tall powerful looking young man teeing off?' 'Yes,' I replied. He had a short backswing but gave the ball an almighty wallop. 'Well that's Brian Barnes from Burnham and Berrow, his mother is caddying for him. He's only eighteen, but he is going to go a long way,' said Stanley. Young Brian Barnes won the Kashmir Cup that day and as Stanley had prophesied, duly went on to greater things as a top professional.

A slim young man with a broad Northcountry accent was on the practise putting green for the Schweppes PGA Championship at Saunton. 'I'm going to knock it around in the low sixties this afternoon,' he announced to anyone who was prepared to listen. 'That will be good enough to win it for me,' he went on. I was watching Tony Jacklin, then a young up and coming, but still relatively unknown assistant professional. Tony had a good round, but not quite good enough to pip the late Guy Wolstenholme – the father of the present top Walker Cup golfer, Gary – who won the Schweppes that day.

The King's Head pub in Northam was a very convenient stopping off place for a quick one, for those leaving the club and heading for Bideford. I was having an animated conversation with 'Dickie' Warmington, the future owner of Warmington's Garage in Bideford, when in walked Christopher Morgan, the very suave son of Captain Morgan (whom I often used to golf with after arranging the game in the dole queue at the Bideford labour exchange). Christopher eventually climbed a few rungs above his father and ended up as Vice Admiral Sir Christopher Morgan. I bought Christopher a drink and introduced him to Dickie; after listening to the conversation for a couple of minutes he said to Dickie, 'How frightfully boring for you,' turned his back on him and ignored him from then on. Christopher was really a very charming gentleman, despite his cruel rebuff of Dickie and had a way with him

45

that made you feel the centre of attention and the only person that mattered in the room at that moment. He was of course patronising to a degree, but great fun to be with and it was easy to see how he had reached the higher echelons of the Royal Navy.

Chapter Eight
Rhodesia

Devon in winter, whilst not as cold as further North, tends to be raw, wet and often overcast for days on end. Having had the sun on my back in Africa and India, each succeeding winter in Devon seemed to get more depressing and I started longing for the wide open spaces and the hot sun again.

Duggie Still was a good friend of mine from Tanganyika days and I started harking back to what he had said to me, 'Chris I come from Rhodesia, it's God's own country – if you ever get the chance to go there, do so. You'll never regret it.'

Carole and I had been married by then for four years; she was a farmer's daughter and loved the Devon countryside and way of life. So when I started applying for jobs in Rhodesia, she just laughed and was happy that I was keeping myself amused. But when I was offered, and accepted, a job as an agricultural advisory officer in the Rhodesian tribal areas, she nearly went berserk. 'If your father had helped us to lease a farm in the county, I would have put my head down and made a show, but he hasn't offered to help. So we're going to Rhodesia and you'll have to make the best of it,' I told her. 'Leave my father out of it,' she shouted. A few hours later, when she had calmed down a bit, she said to me, 'OK then, Rhodesia it is, you're a stubborn old fool, but I presume I'll just have to make the best of it.'

So we arrived in Rhodesia in early January 1972, having sailed out on a Union castle liner which docked at Durban and then we drove up in convoy, with me in a Land Rover and Carole following in a brand new Triumph Herald.

Just after we left I missed a cross-country marathon between Westward Ho! and Saunton, organised by the wonderfully eccentric Geoff Thornton; the same mad hatter with whom Tony Waldeck and I had played in the pouring rain one Easter Meeting. Geoff organised a team of golfers and he himself struck the first blow from the first tee at Westward Ho! then they continued in a straight line across the burrows, to a point where the Taw and Torridge estuary is at its narrowest, so that a ball could be struck across the water when the tide was at its lowest.

This achieved the golfers crossed the water in two pre-arranged rowing boats, manned by local Appledore fishermen and continued across the mudflats, onto the golf course, until finally holing out on Saunton's eighteenth green. I can't remember the number of shots they said they took, but it was well over a thousand and the event caused quite a stir in golfing circles in sleepy North Devon.

Our first posting in Rhodesia was to Mtoko, no more than a small village in English terms, a hundred miles North East of Salisbury the capital with nothing in between the two but bush. A nine-hole golf course, once again with browns instead of greens, had been hacked out of the bush next to the Mtoko club. To get to the third and twelfth tees, you had quite a steep climb up the side of a kopje (those rugged granite hills, such an attractive feature of many parts of Rhodesia). This short climb was no joke for many of the golfers, especially the farmers, many of whom sported enormous stomachs. When they reached the tees, they would stop and pant like a large dog on a very hot day, to get their breath back.

Virtually all the golfers were self-taught and some of the resulting swings had to be seen to be believed, especially those that had to navigate a vast stomach before striking the ball. But they all loved it and the games proceeded midst shouts and hoots of laughter and profane language the likes of which I had never encountered anywhere else before. A holler of 'shag' meant that someone had had a shank and bearing in mind the varied and unusual swings, this was not an infrequent occurrence.

The district magistrate, Clem Lucas, was the most awful golfer I have ever set eyes upon. Unlike the others he took the game very seriously and after each bad shot he would raise his arms and eyes to the sky and say in an anguished voice, 'Why me?' One longed to answer him and say, 'Because you're such a bloody awful golfer.'

After Sunday morning golf big thirsts were slaked in the club bar, whilst rounds were discussed again and legs were pulled; then much later the often equally rotund wives would arrive to drive their men folk home, for a well-earned afternoon zizz.

Mtoko was one of the epicentres of the war, which escalated almost out of control in the late seventies. On one famous occasion, I was told, there was a full-blooded firefight on top of the Kopje between security forces and a gang of terrorists, but despite the proximity of the action to the course, the golfers only abandoned the monthly mug with some reluctance. Mtoko golf was a new and most enjoyable experience for me.

North and east of Mtoko village were the vast expanses of the Tribal areas, which I used to visit each day in my Land Rover, to advise the African farmers and try to improve their primitive agricultural methods. South and west of the village were the white owned farms, where they grew tobacco, maize and sunflower and kept herds of beef cattle – prime Rhodesian beef couldn't be bettered anywhere in the world. At the centre of this white farming area was a farmer's club, much smaller than Mtoko club, called Huyuyu. The farmers decided to build a nine-hole golf course around the club and invited Mtoko people and farmers from further afield, for a grand opening ceremony.

It was in mid November, the hottest month of the year and Huyuyu is at an even lower altitude than Mtoko. So it was just like being in a cauldron when we teed off around noon – as hot as I have ever known it on a golf course. I played with a cheerful, always smiling Afrikaner, called Jan Lombard and the equally pleasant Leon Doré, of Austrian descent, who had a deep guttural voice. Both, probably in their late forties at the time, had massive protruding stomachs, the result of a lifetime of serious overeating. Farmers' wives in both Rhodesia and South Africa seem to have one mission in life and that is to feed their men gargantuan portions of food, which coupled with copious quantities of beer leads to gross obesity and sadly, often an early demise.

We played the first hole without incident, then walked up a steep incline to the second tee. By the time we got there, both those worthies were blowing like puffing Billies and both were puce in the face. There was a bench conveniently placed by the tee which they both gratefully sat down on to regain their breath. It gave way and they hit the ground together. What a comical sight it was to see those two enormous men, both with their legs flailing in the air, just like giant tortoises lying on their backs, trying to right themselves. We were all three in hysterics, as with some difficulty, I helped them to their feet. I still think it's one of the funniest sights I have ever seen.

As much as I liked Mtoko, Carole hated it. So I asked for and was granted, a posting to Goromonzi, only 28 miles east of Salisbury, where

I was made the Senior Agricultural Officer for four small tribal areas – small that is compared to the vastness of the Mtoko Tribal Trust Lands. We lived in Goromonzi until we left Rhodesia for South Africa in late 1978 and when I left tribal agriculture to try my hand at Estate Agency in 1975, we vacated our government house and moved into a vacant farm assistants' house, on the outskirts of the village.

I joined the immaculate Ruwa Golf and Country Club, which was only nine miles down the road towards Salisbury. Ruwa Club was formed after the Second World War by four wealthy farmers, all of whom were still playing golf when I arrived in 1973. Perhaps the doyen of them all was Leslie Cullinan, whose family made their fortune out of diamonds – the 'Cullinan Diamond', being still one of the largest and most valuable precious stones to come out of the big hole at Kimberley. If ever the coffers needed topping up at Ruwa, Leslie would put his hand in his pocket and help out.

As it was only nineteen miles east of Salisbury, on a good tar road, Ruwa had become the favoured club of many a Salisbury businessman. Mostly older men, they would arrive in their Jags and Mercs, tolerate the golf at which most of them didn't exactly shine, then get down to the serious business of the day – good whisky and good conversation. It was through the introduction by Philip Duncan to the managing director of H Shapiro & Co, that I secured the position of farm salesman with that firm, when I decided it was time to leave tribal agriculture. Unbeknown to me, Philip whom I often played with at Ruwa, was the chairman of Shapiro & Co, the leading firm of cattle auctioneers in Mashonaland. Golf as ever, opens so many doors.

'What do you think about that pair?' whispered the young farmer sitting next to me in the changing room, after we have showered. 'Very impressive,' I replied, 'but they must be one hell of an encumbrance to carry around.' The young farmer was referring to a tall old gentleman who had the longest pair of dangling testicles I have ever seen, fully a foot long without any exaggeration. And equally famous at Ruwa was the chap whose vital member was every bit as long as the old boy's testicles.

The parkland course at Ruwa was lined with the most beautiful flat-topped indigenous Msasa trees. In spring (September in Rhodesia) the new leaves unfurled in rustic reds, orange and purple – similar to beech leaves in an English autumn – it was a quite magnificent sight.

A curiosity was the giant bullfrogs which appeared on the course at the height of the rainy season in December. We were walking after our drives up the eleventh fairway, when one of the fourball said to me, 'Have you ever seen a frog as large as that one Chris?' He was pointing to a frog the size of a dinner plate, which was emitting deep, menacing croaks. 'No, I certainly haven't,' I replied, walking over to have a closer look. 'I wouldn't touch it if I were you,' he said. So I gave it a prod with my driver instead, which the brute promptly grabbed and left three ugly scratches on it with its teeth. That was the last time I tangled with a Rhodesian bullfrog.

Other than Ruwa, there were a good number of superb courses dotted around Salisbury, all of which I played on at regular intervals. Little wonder with such perfect golfing conditions throughout the year, that Rhodesia has produced world-class golfers of the calibre of Nick Price, Mark McNulty and Dennis Watson.

'As you are now down to eight handicap, you are eligible for the Rhodesian Amateur,' said John Tabor the secretary at Ruwa, one day in early 1973. I had never played in a seventy-two-hole competition before, so I replied, 'Why not?'

Royal Salisbury was the venue, the course was right next to the leafy jacaranda lined avenues and so close one could hear and almost feel the bustle of city life. Normally it wasn't too difficult a test of the average amateur golfer's talents; but with the tees way back for the 'big one', the rough allowed to grow thick and a foot high, and the carries even to reach the fairway formidable, it had become a monster. It was all really too much for me. But at least I can say I have played in a National Amateur Championship, even if I was the last non-qualifier, for somebody has to be last. A month later Royal Salisbury had decided to commemorate its seventy-fifth anniversary by inviting Royal Clubs from around the world for a week long festival and celebration. Normally golf clubs celebrate centenaries, not shorter periods of time. Was it perhaps with the escalating bush war in the country in mind, that the club had a gut feeling that it would no longer be called Royal Salisbury when the centenary celebration would be due in 1998? If so, how right they were, as it very quickly became Royal Harare in the early 1980s.

My home club, Royal North Devon (I was an overseas member), was a man short and I didn't need any persuasion to make up the numbers, especially as my wife was in England at the time. Our three-man team consisted of 'Bucket' Cole and me, the third member I think a Dr Blakey from New Zealand, also an overseas member of RND, didn't turn up. Bucket had married Judy Harman, daughter of the Harman family of Northam Post Office and they were living in Johannesburg when he answered the call. Why 'Bucket' I can't remember, but they were certainly good company. A round of golf every day on that splendid course, followed by a reception every evening after golf!

We were well into our second gin-and-tonics, when a familiar face edged into our circle. 'How did your rounds go today?' said Prime Minister Ian Smith in his clipped Rhodesian accent. His official residence was only a few hundred yards from the clubhouse and he had slipped into the reception unannounced and at first unnoticed. 'Most enjoyable day, sir,' Bucket and I chorused on cue. It was the first time either of us had met him in the flesh. 'Which part of the world do the two of you come from?' he asked. When he realised we were locals representing our English clubs he was soon chatting away, about golf, sport in general and Rhodesia. Bucket, Judy and I stood transfixed and listened to this slight, intense man, with the wavy lock of hair falling over his forehead, tell us of his future hopes for his beloved Rhodesia.

'Ian, are you talking to the Westward Ho! contingent?' asked the President's wife, Armanella du Pont. She sailed into our circle with her retinue following attentively in her wake – a fulsome woman, very sure of herself as the wife of the President of Rhodesia. ' You won't remember me, ma'am. I'm a bit younger than you,' I said. 'I was brought up at Wellesbourne, not three hundred yards from your family home and once, as a small boy, I bought a sitting of hen eggs from your mother,' I continued.

'Oh, I remember Wellesbourne and the Stapledons who lived there before you. How wonderful to meet Westward Ho! people again. Clifford,' she called across the room to her husband, 'come over here, darling, and meet some people from North Devon, my home.' The President of Rhodesia duly came over. He was a small man with a moustache, much older than her, for she had come to Rhodesia as a nurse and had married the future President, after nursing him through a difficult illness. He was a quiet, dignified man who spoke with a guttural Afrikaans accent, for I believe he originally came from South Africa. The 'Bucket' Coles and Christopher Land, certainly had had quite some evening. Altogether a most memorable week's golf.

'You stay here and mark my ball,' for it was partly obscured in the semi-rough, 'and I'll go and help find the boss's ball,' I said to my caddy.

It was the Salisbury South Open, held one October, the hottest and driest time of the year and the rough was tinder dry. Whilst I was away, helping to search for the lost ball, the caddy had apparently lit a cigarette, had thrown the match away which ignited the grass around him, and the resulting fire spread rapidly, and was soon out of control. There he stood gaping at my golf bag, which was already burning merrily. I screamed at him, 'Get my bag out, you bloody fool.'

This galvanised him into action; he leapt into the flames, grabbed the bag and managed to put out the fire, though the leather grips were still smouldering an hour later. A major bush fire quickly enveloped the course and the billowing clouds of acrid blinding smoke caused the cancellation of the competition. 'Which bloody fool caused that lot?' was the angry question on many lips, when all the golfers had trudged back to the clubhouse. As each golfer is responsible for his caddy, it was incumbent on me to own up. 'I did,' I said, with a nervous sheepish grin. I can tell you, I wasn't a particularly popular visitor to Salisbury South that day, to say the least.

There were never more than 280,000 whites, men, women and children in Rhodesia, so there was a good chance if you played in the open competitions, that you would sometimes meet some of the 'big boys'. I played in the Mashonaland Open Foursomes one year and after we had finished our round, we walked back to the last match to watch Price, Watson and McNulty – all of whom were young emerging amateurs at the time – play the last few holes. I won a rocking chair in the 'Springmaster Furniture Company Open' (they were prominent sponsors of Rhodesian golf), by topping the 'B' division and I remember Simon Hobday was the leading professional that day. Because of British sanctions against Rhodesia, Simon had very limited travel options to ply his trade as a tournament professional, so he could usually be found in the bar at Chapman Golf Club in Salisbury, always with a cigarette between his lips and a bottle of beer at hand. He was a real character.

The Rhodesian Open was played at Chapman in 1977; the then Ruwa Club champion Graham Kileff, kindly invited me to make up a four in a practise round the day before the competition proper. The others were Mike Reinders, one of the best amateurs in the country and Gary

Player's protégé, the professional Peter Matkovitch – who never quite fulfilled the promise that Gary saw in him. It was a wonderful experience and it brought home to me the enormous gulf there was between myself off eight handicap, a top amateur and a good professional. But the beauty of golf is that it is one of the few games where, because of the handicap system and the fact that each golfer plays his own ball, one can theoretically have a chance against the best; unlike say tennis or squash, where one would be lucky to ever win a point against the top players.

The great South African golfer, Gary Player and his friend the New Zealand southpaw, Bob Charles, gave a clinic followed by an exhibition round at Royal Salisbury in the mid seventies. Gary was still very much a force to be reckoned with in world golf and was destined to win yet another major; Bob Charles was the only left-hander to have won 'The Open'; which he achieved in 1963. Mainly because of Gary's popularity and fame, especially in Southern Africa, a very big crowd turned up that day.

Gary was dressed all in yellow I remember, instead of his more customary black attire and he immediately struck up a wonderful empathy with the crowd. He had a microphone wired up, which was threaded up his trouser leg, and through his shirtfront, so that he could talk whilst at the same time demonstrating during the clinic. One wag from the crowd said, 'Be careful that wire cable doesn't do you a damage Gary.' Gary laughed and was quick as a flash with a witty reply.

At the conclusion of the most informative clinic, Gary told us all that they were going to try a trick that they had worked on together. It was so audacious that I still marvel at their sheer nerve to even try it. Gary said, 'Right, ladies and gentlemen, Bob and I are going to try to get two golf balls to touch each other in mid air.' Each stood with a wedge facing each other (not forgetting that Bob was a left-hander) approximately fifteen feet apart. Gary then said, 'One, two, three,' and then he and Bob simultaneously hit full wedge shots. At the top of their trajectories the two balls actually came within a foot of each other, but when they tried it for a second time, the two balls touched in mid air. There was instantaneous applause and shouts of approval. In retrospect, I suppose the fact that the balls got so close to touching the first time was amazing in itself; but when they touched in mid air at the second attempt, it was a feat of exceptional skill and considerable daring.

Chapter Nine
Down South

Her eyes were laughing at me and her tongue lolling out of the side of her mouth, as she sat behind the Secretary's chair in his office at Port Shepstone Country Club. 'She pitched up at the club in early January,' said the Secretary. 'She was probably dumped by 'Vaalies' (holiday makers from the Transvaal), at the end of their Christmas holidays – they just leave their pets behind,' he said, angrily shaking his head. 'You can have her if you look after her, she's very affectionate, they even bothered to have her spayed.' 'She's just the sort of dog we've been looking for. I'd love to have her.' I replied. We called her Sophie – a big yellow shaggy dog – probably a cross between a Labrador and an Irish Wolfhound. She was wonderful with my two young daughters. 'She's been having a round of golf a day with the members, sometimes two and they have quickly grown very fond of her,' said the Secretary.

We arrived in Port Shepstone just before Christmas 1978 and one of the very generous perks that formed part of my contract as a salesman with Aubrey Thompson Estate Agents, was membership of the local golf club. We left Rhodesia because it had become patently obvious that majority rule was inevitable and I have always refused to live under incompetent and corrupt black rule. So, 'Down South' we moved where I was sure the ruling Nationalist party dominated by the Afrikaner, would never hand over to majority rule. Yet again I was proved wrong!

Port Shepstone is 100 miles down the coast from Durban, in the hot and humid Natal South Coast. The golf course there was most unusual, in that the first nine holes was parkland surrounded by thick riverine bush, airless hot and humid; the second nine holes was an open links layout affected by the vagaries of the seaside winds and as different as chalk and cheese to the first nine. Only once did I in any way come to terms with the course in five years of endeavour and the engraved monthly mug I won is now one of my proudest possessions.

The Umzimkulu river has it's source high in the Drakensburg mountains some 300 miles inland, but it is wide, sluggish and often menacing, as it passes the golf course with the Indian Ocean in sight.

There is a plaque on the wall of the main bar, marking the height of the flood waters, when the river broke its banks in 1956 and flooded the course and clubhouse, to a depth of six feet.

The caddy looked at me and I looked at the caddy. He looked at me again and I looked back at him, but still nothing happened. My second wife, Marina could not be described as even remotely sports orientated, quite the opposite; but on the premise that if you can't beat 'em you might as well join 'em, she had decided to take up golf. Perhaps nearly a minute passed – it certainly seemed like it – before a shot was played and then inevitably it was a fresh air shot, as were the next four or five swipes which followed. We were on holiday at the Drakensburg Gardens Hotel, situated directly beneath the awesome towering mountain range which marks the border between Lesotho and South Africa. It was a tortuous nine holes on this lovely scenic course and the first and last that Marina played. 'I hate the game, I shall never master it and I never want to go through that sort of humiliation again,' she said almost in tears. 'But the caddy doesn't mind, all he cares about is the money he gets at the end of the round,' I pleaded. But that was it and she never played again. For some people, lacking in coordination and not good at ball games, golf is a fiendishly difficult game.

There is another fine course at Underberg in the same district as the one mentioned above, further out from the mighty Drakensburg mountain range, which offers more distant views of Lesotho and it is devastatingly beautiful when covered in blankets of sparkling white snow in winter. When you turn off the tar into Underberg Club, you are greeted by an avalanche of shouting, laughing caddies, who rush up to your car pleading, 'Me boss, me boss, me very good caddy, boss.' You choose one of these half-naked scruffy individuals and the rest rush off to clamour around the next car that pulls in. 'What's your name?' you ask. 'Lovemore, boss.' 'Right, Lovemore, there are six golf balls in this bag.' You count the balls out in front of him, otherwise they are likely to mysteriously disappear before the end of the round. As your game gets underway, so the caddies quickly size you up and bet between themselves on the outcome of the match. If you are having a bad day, your caddy will rapidly lose interest in you, the impish smile will leave his face, for the chances are that nearly all of his caddy fee at the end of the game will go to pay out the bets with his fellow caddies. This scenario is played out every Saturday afternoon throughout South Africa on the more remote country courses, where the caddies are invariably impoverished labourer's sons from the nearby 'location' (African township).

At the larger plusher courses – near the towns and cities – the caddies are always controlled by a caddy master (an older African appointed by the club) and are usually kept in a pen and let out as required. Demeaning and demoralising for the poor fellows, a foreign visitor would say, but a fact of life in South Africa, where there are vast numbers of Africans, rampant inflation and massive unemployment. Thirty, forty years ago everyone had a caddy, now only the very wealthy and overseas visitors who benefit from the favourable rand exchange rate, can afford one. The majority of golfers these days either pull their own trolley, own a battery powered buggie, or often two golfers will club together and hire an electrified golf cart from the pro, cheaper and less hassle than a caddy.

Unlike England, you won't often find golf balls during a round in South Africa. The ground staff and itinerant unemployed caddies, search for lost balls and then much to the annoyance of the club professional they will accost you on the course, 'Want to buy golf balls boss, only ten rand boss, please boss,' they will implore you. Far cheaper than the pro's shop and ten rand for an unemployed African is a fortune. On courses with water you will often see Africans sometimes immersed up to their necks in the water. They will probably be completely naked, their coal black skins glistening with droplets and they will wade slowly across the lake or dam, feeling for balls with their toes, then when they have located one they will dive to the bottom and pick it up. They reap a rich harvest of golf balls this way. Occasionally a caddy will disappear without trace, becoming a good meal for a hungry crocodile, for on some courses crocodiles abound; but he will soon be forgotten and his place taken by another – that is the way of Africa.

Speeding along the freeway between the Lower South Coast and Durban you will often see little black boys holding up plastic bags full of golf balls to attract your attention. They will have found them in the rough of a plush new golf course which runs parallel with the freeway. If you were to stop to buy some balls, you may also be offered a crayfish, illegally caught amongst the rock pools in the sea nearby. But watch out! There are very heavy fines if you are caught by the Police with a live crayfish, and no licence for it.

'What's that circle of red flags over there for?' I asked one of the locals during a round at Jeffreys Bay – near Port Elizabeth. 'That's to guard a Crowned Plover's nest,' he said. 'They lay their four beautiful blotched eggs in a shallow scrape on the ground, often on the fairway or in the semi rough. There are three or four nests on the course marked like that,' he said. I went over to have a closer look and the hen bird slunk quietly off the nest to reveal four perfectly camouflaged eggs, whilst her mate flew agitatedly around warning me off. There were four, 4" long stakes stuck in the ground, each with a red flag attached to it. 'The flags are remarkably effective, they will all probably rear their young successfully – the only danger is a direct hit on the nest by a ball – fortunately this rarely happens,' he said.

Bird life is abundant on all the golf courses in South Africa. There are Egyptian Geese, black and white Blacksmith Plovers – their call similar to a blacksmith striking an anvil – beautiful bronze, black and white streaked African Jacanas with prehensile toes, which enable them to walk on lily pads floating in the dams, a tree full of Weavers nests, not unlike a Christmas tree covered in presents and many others which add such interest to the round for the keen golfing ornithologist.

Royal Port Alfred in the Eastern Cape, between Port Elizabeth and East London, is one of the 'Royal five' of Southern Africa. Royal Harare (Royal Salisbury when I played there), Royal Johannesburg, Royal Durban and Royal Cape, make up the other four – they have a royal meeting each year at one of the five courses. I have played Royal Port Alfred, set in the heart of 1820 settler country many times. It's a wonderful test of golf, a links course with fearsome bush surrounding most fairways and the constant roar of the Indian Ocean breakers, in the background. The intrepid 1820 settlers sailed out from England in wooden sailing ships, as they were surplus to requirements once the Napoleonic Wars were over and each family went out with the promise of rich virgin land to settle and farm. However, they were conveniently not told that the fierce warrior Xhosa tribe considered the Eastern Cape their homeland and many settlers lost their lives in the ensuing battles with the natives, until land tenure was finally sorted out. The descendants of those original settlers have formed a very English enclave in the Eastern Cape and are very proud to tell you they come from settler stock.

At the highest point of the course on the third fairway, you can sometimes see a whale rearing out of the water and arching its back to the sky and fishermen fish with lights from small boats to attract and catch the South African culinary delicacy called calamari or choka, which in Europe is known as squid or octopus.

The Marquard nine hole golf course on the outskirts of the dorp (small village) of that name in remote Eastern Orange Free State, is so typical of the country golf course in South Africa. I was staying on a large farm nearby with Stefan and Jenny Jacobsz, Stefan as Afrikaner as they come said, 'Come Chris man, it's Saturday, we'll join in the competition this afternoon.' The Orange Free State seems to be a breeding ground for Springbok front row forwards like him. He was built like the proverbial brick shithouse. Stefan was probably only about 5'9" tall, he must have weighed sixteen stone at least; his arms and legs were as thick as tree stumps and he had a short bull neck which descended into awesome broad shoulders. He was the very last person I would ever argue with!

So we went to golf and his fellow Afrikaner farmer friends came up to greet the 'Engelsman' staying with Stefan Jacobsz. Each in turn solemnly grasped my hand in their massive paws and with a vice like grip introduced themselves as, 'Lombard, de Klerk, Pienaar, Moolman,' etc etc. It felt as though my hand had been pulped as I reached the first tee and tried to grip my driver. Like the Mtoko farmers in Rhodesia many of them had enormous protruding stomachs and likewise were mostly self-taught. When they made contact, which didn't always happen, the ball remained hit, huge divots would fly through the air and the ground seemed to shake beneath our feet.

The coals in the braai fires (barbecues) would already be glowing red by the time we finished the round, awaiting the chops, steaks and boerewors (a delicious Afrikaans sausage). Then bottle after bottle of 'Castle' lager was consumed, to quench the thirst and enhance the waistline. Those trips to the Eastern Orange Free State were very happy occasions and although I can speak only a smattering of Afrikaans, golf as ever united us.

During the last seven years of my time in South Africa, I lived in Simon's Town – near the old British naval dockyard, twenty-five miles south of that wondrous city, Cape Town, with Table Mountain towering above it – and close to the last stopping off place in Africa, Cape Point. Sir Francis Drake is reputed to have described it as, 'The fairest Cape in all the world,' and I would certainly agree with him. I was a member of immaculate Clovelly Country Club, close to Simon's Town and my office at nearby Fish Hoek. I used to wear my Clovelly shirts and jerseys back in England before the small North Devon course came into being. 'Yer boy,' the locals would say down in Cornwall, 'us didn't know there was a 'course up in Clovelly, cor bugger.' I managed to string them along for quite some time.

Like Salisbury in Rhodesia there are some fine championship courses around Cape Town – real tests for the very best golfers, especially when the ferocious prevailing south-easter blows in summer. At one of them – Royal Cape, one of the legs of the South African Sunshine Circuit – I met John Daly. He was then an unknown professional at the start of his career and was playing with Donald Gammon, whose father 'Mus' was the pro at Chapman in Salisbury. My wife and I walked around with them for a few holes – we were their only gallery – and funnily enough I can't remember Daly being a particularly big hitter. Whilst they were waiting to tee off on a short hole I asked John, 'Why is it that pro's never play with yellow golf balls?' 'Well,' he drawled in his marked yankee accent, 'next time you use a yellow ball, see how the yellow hue reflects onto the shaft. It's distracting, that's why we pro's don't use them.' He gave us a warm smile and although I missed out a few years later in backing him as an unknown 'rookie' when he won the US PGA; I more than made up for it when I backed him at generous odds in the 'Open' of 1995, when he pipped Costantino Rocca in a play off, to win the famous claret jug.

I have never met Ernie Els, but saw him once as a teenager on the practise putting green at Stellenbosch golf club (30 miles to the east of the Cape Peninsula) and at the same time he was chatting up the young teenage girls. As youngsters, he and Ben Fouché couldn't be separated, they were such outstanding talents. Then suddenly Ernie shot ahead and became the international star that he is today, while poor old Ben never progressed any further. Ben's main claim to fame was winning a dozen cases of whisky for a hole in one, in a tournament sponsored by 'Bells' at Mowbray golf course in Cape Town.

On the fringe of Stellenbosch golf course is a 'Shebeen' (a drinking house) where the locals go to drink a very potent locally brewed beer. Virtually all the workers in and around the Cape Peninsula and those employed on the vineyards near Stellenbosch, are 'Cape coloureds' – a happy go lucky mixed race. Four of us had reached a short hole, where the ground falls away steeply to the green down below, when a man came weaving out from the direction of the shebeen, careering from side to side and talking loudly to himself. He just made the green and then collapsed full length on it. We shouted 'Fore' to him and other unprintables, without any show of recognition or further movement on his part. So we all played our tee shots and walked down to the green, when he somehow managed to stagger to his feet, swaying violently and said, 'Hello bossee, sorry bossee,' and then fell flat on his face again, this time out for the count. We putted around his prostrate body, pulled him off the green and left him there to sleep it off. Definitely one of the funnier sights I have seen on a golf course.

I started this book at Ceres up in the mountains north of Cape Town, where Richard Davidson had shouted 'Fore' to a troupe of baboons ambling across a fairway. In the Ceres clubhouse a circle of us were having a convivial drinks session together after a game and took turns in buying a round each. I noticed an Afrikaans Dominee (a vicar in the strict church, that all Afrikaners attend without fail on Sundays) was the recipient of a drink every time, but quite obviously had no intention of standing a round himself. When it came to my turn to buy a round, I pointedly left him out, 'What about me?' he said in his limited clipped English. 'What about you!' I said. 'You buy the next round, then and only then will I buy you a drink.' He was flustered and the Afrikaners present embarrassed. It underlines the absolute power, bordering on fear, which the Dominee traditionally held and still holds over his flock. The Dominee sees to their spiritual future and they fork out for his creature comforts, so he never has to put his hand into his own pocket. This deep-seated approach to religion would seem to have been the achilles heel of the Afrikaner. I have read most of the definitive books on the history of the Boer War. All seem to agree that had General Joubert – the Supreme Commander of the Boer forces, a God-fearing Afrikaner, well into his sixties – listened to his younger generals, they would probably have won the Boer War. At the start of the war in Natal, with the British out of their depth in a foreign country and in retreat, had the Boers pressed on they would have driven them into the sea. But the good general called a halt to the rout, as it was a Sunday and a day of prayer, which allowed the British to regroup in Ladysmith and eventually, as history records, win the war.

Chapter Ten
The Full Circle

Stretching out from the holiday village of Perranporth on the North coast of Cornwall are three miles of golden sands. But at high tide if you want to continue your walk, you have to climb the headland and follow the cliff top path. Then you see golfers, with the course so close to the cliff edge, that you could almost imagine yourself tumbling down the sheer rock face onto the sand far below.

'This looks like our sort of course,' I said to my wife Gill. 'Yes, but I bet it's wild in winter when the wind blows,' she replied. 'And it's so exposed,' she continued. 'Can you imagine what it will be like playing when the wind blows the rain in from the sea – you won't be able to stand up.' 'I know, I know, but I used to love it at Westward Ho! when the wind blew the drizzle into your face and you walked on the fine springy grasses. Let's walk across the course darling, and have a chat with the Secretary.' 'OK, but it will only be an enquiry,' she said. 'We're still in temporary accommodation, you haven't got a permanent job and until you get one, we can't even think of playing golf. It will be far too expensive,' she said, ever the practical one, compared to my headstrong happy-go-lucky approach.

It was June 1992, flaming June and we'd only been back from South Africa two months. South Africa was about to go the same way as Rhodesia (now Zimbabwe); that is the hand over to majority rule and then like Zimbabwe watch the country slowly go down hill to eventual third world standing. It was too heartbreaking and depressing to contemplate – so we left. I said to Gill, who was born and brought up in Surrey, 'Where shall we go?' 'I really don't care,' she replied, for it had been on my instigation that we left South Africa, leaving all her family behind. 'Right,' I said, 'we'll live in Cornwall. I worked down there in the sixties and much as I like North Devon, I'm not really a home town boy, so let's head for pastures new.' That's how we ended up in Cornwall.

For the first six months we lived in a holiday chalet complex in a leafy coombe close to Perranporth and listened for the cuckoo and to the glorious liquid notes of the willow warbler and wood warbler high in the treetops. In July we found a mushroom field, which we visited every day and then the first blackberries started ripening and I did temporary jobs and I got the sack from one, which was an unpleasant novelty for me. Suddenly the winter arrived and the chalet was freezing, we just had to find somewhere to buy and quickly. Our luck held, we bought at the bottom of the market – if we'd left our departure from South Africa much longer we wouldn't have made it, we would have undoubtedly gone under. We are seven miles from Truro and the same distance from Perranporth Golf Club. Our furniture and personal effects including golf clubs had arrived by sea freight, so we joined the club and started playing in September, only five months after our return.

'Shall we enter the Open Winter Foursomes?' I asked Gill. 'It's any combination, man or woman and we will get plenty of shots.' 'I don't think we stand a chance, but I suppose we could give it a go if you really want to,' she replied. We had won more than one prestigious mixed competition together before we left Cape Town and I secretly fancied our chances. I had of course conveniently forgotten that playing in shorts and shirt with the sun on your back, was a little different from playing in two jerseys plus waterproofs in wind and rain, in an English winter. We lost heavily in the first round of the competition proper and then again in the first round of the plate. We were drawn against Derek Michell and Peter Trew, respectively the Perranporth Club Professional and the club's best amateur, who a few years after was to set the course record of 62, a brilliant score unlikely ever to be beaten. I seem to remember we lost 9&7, managing a fortuitous half somewhere along the way. 'How often does this happen?' I asked Derek. We had only played five holes, when banks of fog came rolling in from the sea, blanketing the course and reducing visibility to no more than 50 yards. 'Often,' he replied, smiling broadly, 'you have to get used to it at Perranporth.' It persisted for the remainder of the round and gave Gill and I a partial excuse for such a poor showing.

Perranporth is not long by any means – in fact there isn't one par four over 400 yards – but it's the wind factor virtually throughout the year, that makes the course such a fearsome test of golf. It breaks visitors' hearts and when locals ask, 'Where do you play your golf?' and you reply, 'Perranporth,' it invokes surprise, admiration or even pity, it has such an awesome reputation.

The prevailing wind is from the south-west, but it regularly blows from all the other points of the compass and can swing round as much as

180º during a game. A past club captain, about eight years ago, was successful in applying to the EGU to have the course rating raised by a shot to 73, purely on the wind factor alone. Indeed two or three times a year a competition has to be abandoned because the ball will not remain still on the green. That's how hard it can blow.

I remember one November monthly medal, when the best 'A' division score was 95 gross by Chris Jeffrey playing off 5 handicap and only four golfers broke 100 that day – the wind was as near gale force as makes no difference. Yet on a very rare still day, the course is virtually defenceless to a good golfer. The greens are vintage links, lightning fast and true and despite irrigation a dry spell can make some of them almost unplayable. We had reached the 5th green in a mixed competition one day and the four in front of us were waiting behind the green grinning like fools. 'What are you people waiting for?' I said, 'If you don't get a move on you'll soon be holding up the whole field.' 'We want to watch your next putt Chris, we know what a good putter you are,' they chorused, tongue in cheek. I was above the hole, I only touched the ball with my putter to get it moving – it was a good putt but just lipped out, it then picked up speed and eventually stopped ten yards off the green close to the water hazard, accompanied by ribald laughter from the 6th fairway. 'Better luck next time, Chris,' they said and moved off laughing amongst themselves.

A visitor will say, 'There are too many blind shots,' and you as a member will reply, 'yes, but when you get to know them and where to aim, they will add interest to your round. Persevere, you'll grow to like it here,' and they will walk away with a wry smile on their face, obviously wondering if you are still in possession of all your faculties. But if all else fails the views are breathtaking; stand on the 5th or 14th tees and look west, you can just see St Ives in the distance and in between the rugged coastline with the foam capped breakers smashing against the sheer rock face. My friends will say as we wait to tee off, 'We don't care where in the world you've been Chris, you won't find a finer view than this,' and I have to agree with them.

The course is treeless except for a few small dwarfed hawthorns, almost bent double by the merciless prevailing wind and the rough is impenetrable marram grass and dense patches of brambles. The two Mitchell brothers – Billy and John and their assistant Fred – have been the greenkeepers for almost as long as anyone can remember. They love the course and consequently look after it well, so that it is as much a nature reserve as a golf course. I always like to think I do my bit. I'm the self appointed collector of litter during every round I play. I pick it up, put it in my pocket, then deposit it in the next waste bin. It provokes endless amusement amongst my fellow golfers and it seems it will be a never ending pastime, for the dropping of litter has become endemic. I was ordering a round of drinks at the bar recently whilst the Captain John Stanforth was making his opening speech at the start of his year of office, 'Will Chris Land please come forward for a special presentation,' he said. Much laughter followed from the packed members lounge, for I'm sure they all had an inkling of what it was. I opened a long narrow carefully wrapped parcel and took out a 'litter picker', it brought the house down. I thanked John with a deep bow and grinned from ear to ear.

Spraying for weeds is kept to an absolute minimum and then only on the fairways, the rough remains in its natural untouched state. So wild flowers abound – buttercups in early spring and sea pink on the steep bank above the 4th green, followed by a sea of yellow cowslips – to gladden the eye after a long dark and wet winter. Spring also brings out patches of sweet violets in the rough where rabbits have nibbled the grass down and yellow hawkbit on long waving stalks, take the place of buttercups in the summer. In early summer also vetch and trefoil and the aptly named hay rattle, which when it has seeded and died, rustles like hay in the rough as you search for your ball. Glorious vivid patches of blood red geranium near the 6th tee and the rare pyramid orchid, mauve and pyramid shaped, are a delight. All summer the ragwort is growing (that poisonous plant, particularly to horses), but it is kept under control and sufficient left growing to sustain the striking red and black cinnabar moth and its similar coloured striped caterpillar, which voraciously feed upon it.

Then in high summer banks of sweet smelling wild thyme thrive on the fairways and in the semi rough and the brambles flower and fruit – what pleasure to have a handful of unpolluted blackberries to help you on your way. Evening primrose grows behind the 18th tee – a tall plant with branches of gaudy yellow flowers – I saw the identical plant in the Drakensburg mountains in South Africa, from where I presume the English variety originates.

John Mitchell, who is out at first light to cut the greens, says he regularly sees the fox family that live in the impenetrable bramble above the 5th fairway and an old boar badger makes the course its home in the winter. Rabbits abound and it is not unusual to lose your ball in a rabbit scrape in the middle of the fairway and sometimes a shot will go full tilt straight down a rabbit hole and that's probably the last you will see of that ball – you can try the length of your arm holding a long iron and still you are unlikely to be able to reach it, the burrows are so deep. 'I saw an old dog stoat kill two full grown rabbits within half an hour on the 5th fairway last week,' John Mitchell told me. 'Yes, I've seen the same stoat myself,' I replied. 'He killed the rabbits, drank their blood and then the crows and magpies arrived to finish the carcass off, in no time there was only skin and bone left,' he said. 'They are only doing what the hyena, jackal and vultures do, after the lion has killed and had his fill in Africa,' I told him.

I put my fingers to my lips and pointed to attract Peter Bayly's attention. It was the June monthly medal on a glorious Sunday morning and we had just topped the rise halfway up the fairway on the 17th. There in front of us was a family of six stoats – the youngsters gambling and frolicking in the sunshine around their parents – what a wonderful sight and suddenly how unimportant the game seemed.

If you are a keen bird watcher as well as a golfer, then Perranporth Golf Club is a must. You will always see a kestrel, hovering above the rough – almost still however strong the wind – then it will plummet down and a vole or a mouse will end its short stay on this earth, crushed by the bird's cruel talons. The skylark, dwindling elsewhere in the country, abounds and when in early summer a speckled brown bird scurries from right under your feet in the rough, the chances are that it will have been sitting on a nest, with four grey/brown heavily blotched eggs in it. You eagerly await the first swallows and martins; they will come from the west sometime in March, flying low above the ground, having just returned from their winter sojourn in South Africa. Then in the autumn you ask Billy Mitchell, 'How many swallows nests have you had this year in the machinery shed?' 'Two pairs and each have hatched three broods and we've had a pied wagtail's nest this year and we've seen the barn owl, but they haven't nested yet,' he replied. 'Say hello to our swallows if you see them in South Africa this winter Chris, will you,' he chuckled. 'Yes, I will,' and we smile at each other.

The last time I heard a cuckoo was in May four years ago down in the marsh close to Perranporth village – sadly they are becoming scarce. There's always a flock of rooks on the course diligently searching for cutworms and leather jackets, they come from a large rookery in Perrancoombe a mile away and the course is their main feeding ground. 'They make a hell of a mess with their beaks digging up the fairways, tees and greens, looking for insects,' I once said to Billy, 'It must be one of your major problems.' 'Yes,' he replied, but true countryman that he is, 'we've all got to live, haven't we?' he smiled.

Carrion crows, jackdaws and seagulls are ever present and mob the poor old kestrel and unmercifully harry the buzzards when they come soaring over the course looking for food. Young seagulls will pick up your golf balls in their beaks and play with them and sometimes fly away with them and drop them on other parts of the course. It's infuriating – if you don't see it happen - it's a lost ball and it always seems to occur when you have played a blind shot and you are doing well in a competition.

One year in early February my good friend Ren Jupp said, 'Look at that big black bird, it's got your ball Chris.' It was a raven, it picked up my ball and flew straight out to the cliffs with it, no doubt to put it in it's nest with it's own eggs – I hope it's still sitting on it!

On a wild windy day, to me there is no finer melody than a pair of ravens calling to each other with their lovely cronking note, as they pass high overhead. A bird of the rugged cliffs and lonely seashore, we are fortunate to have the ravens in these parts.

When winter comes the meadow pippit and linnet join the skylarks in small flocks on the fairways, feeding on grass and weed seeds and a wily old cock pheasant makes the course his home when the shooting season starts, knowing perhaps that the course is never shot over. One year a lone oyster-catcher appeared on the 10th fairway and stayed there for a couple of months and next to the practise putting green, is a thick stunted hawthorn, not more than three feet high, where the magpies nest each spring. And finally the wheatear, that harbinger of spring and autumn, arrives in April and can be seen sitting on the edge of a rabbit hole, bobbing its tail up and down when you come near it – then departing for the moors where it breeds, only to return again to the same rabbit holes on the practise ground, in September.

Chapter Eleven
Perran

Bob McGregor, the Perranporth Club Chairman said, 'Chris, I want you to meet our new Secretary David Mugford.' 'How do you do,' I said rather formally as we shook hands. 'I hope you have a long enjoyable association with the club. What part of the country do you come from David?' 'Torquay,' he replied. 'Oh, I know Torquay well, I've played the course several times and Torquay used to be one of my old stomping grounds years ago, when I was at agricultural college near Newton Abbot.' 'How long have you been a member here, Chris?' David asked me. 'About eight years I think. I'm sure you are going to find it a very good golf course, one of a number of good ones in the county, you're going to enjoy it here,' I replied.

Before settling in Cornwall, I had only played St Enedoc (with my old friend David Pennington) and West Cornwall in the far west – another excellent links course – with my father in 1964. Since then I have added most of the other courses in the county to the list. Gill and I have always played in the 'Garfield Daniels' Open Mixed Foursomes at West Cornwall in late April each year. One year we won it. On the first tee the year we won, I said to our playing partners, 'You're in the two club of course, shall we share as usual?' 'No we haven't entered, the chances of getting a two are so slim, it's a complete waste of money,' they said. As luck would have it, Gill and I had the only two that day as well and we won 84 golf balls (7 boxes). Our partners looked so crestfallen at the prize giving, that I felt sorry for them and gave them a box. Gill was furious, 'Why give a box of balls to them – they were too mean to enter – they don't even deserve one ball each.' 'Oh come, Darling,' I replied, 'surely it doesn't do any harm to share our good fortune.' We agreed to differ, but agreed we had had a memorable day.

I returned to Cornwall with a 12 handicap but before I got to know the wiles of Perranporth that first winter, I slipped out to 14, the highest I had been for many years. John Thomas, Club Captain in 1993/4 said to me, 'Chris, I'm putting you in the Cornish Bowl side to partner Stan Dean. With your experience and Stan's comparative youth and strength, the two of you as top couple, should be good for a banker point.' 'Fine,' I replied. 'Who are we playing and where?' 'We're playing Falmouth at

Tehidy,' said John. The Cornish Bowl is a knockout foursomes competition played annually by all golf clubs in Cornwall and is for handicaps of 13 or over. There are five pairs in each team and it starts in October and the final, if you get through all the rounds, is the following April.

Tehidy Park, towards the coast from Camborne, is a typical parkland course with lush fairways and lots of trees lining most holes. The park was originally the home of the Bassett family, who made their fortune in the distant past from tin mining. The imposing mansion still stands on the edge of the course and the mile long driveway criss-crosses the fairways up to the fine front portico.

What John Thomas hadn't of course realised was that he had put together two Sagittarians – excitable and headstrong – with that often disastrous tendency for acting first and thinking later. I don't know about Stan, but I certainly didn't sleep a wink the night before, I was so nervous.

'I'll take the tee shot on the 1st,' Stan said to me, obviously under extreme pressure. We shook hands with our opponents and then Stan wound himself up and to his eternal credit, hit a massive drive which unfortunately drifted just off the fairway into thick lush grass, not more than a sand wedge from the green. He came running down the fairway all pumped up and justly proud of himself and said excitedly in his broad Mancunian accent, 'Anywhere on the green Chris mate, all you have to do is just nudge it on,' for we both knew that our opponents had started badly. 'Will do,' I said and promptly hit my favourite shot under pressure, a shank, which went ten yards deeper into the rough. We lost that hole and the comedy of errors continued, until we shook hands again well out in the country and well beaten.

I shall always remember the Stanley classic at the 12th, when we still had a vague chance of pulling the game round. The 12th hole at Tehidy is a long par five, with out of bounds all the way down the right hand side. I had hit my tee shot well and also well away from the dreaded out of bounds; before I could reach him to discuss tactics, Stan had taken out his three wood and had hit an enormous second shot in completely the wrong direction. For it cleared the out of bounds fence still rising and went so far into the woods that it is probably still there now, for nobody would think of looking for a golf ball that far in.

The captain came over and smiled and shook our hands, 'Bad luck, lads,' he said. But he knew and we knew that we had made a nonsense and had thrown it away.

Winter league has become an institution at Perranporth on a winter Saturday. The format is always fourball better ball stableford and there is a draw each week for partners, so that you never get the same partner more than once, between October and March, when it finishes with a grand prize giving and a free meal. It was certainly a novelty to me when we returned from overseas, but I gather it was started some sixteen years ago and now most clubs in Cornwall have a winter league. 'Only five months to the start of winter league,' people would say and then as it drew nearer, 'winter league starts in six weeks time – I saw old Osborne out practising yesterday – sure sign that it's just around the corner.' 'He's a pot hunter if ever there was one,' said Ren. 'I agree,' I said, 'but we'd certainly miss it if there wasn't a game each Saturday, it's the highlight of the week, good old Peter and Fred.' We were unanimous that they did a sterling job in organising it.

Another excellent innovation that a past Captain introduced seven years ago is the Tuesday medal/stableford. One week it is a medal competition and the next a stableford, always played off back tees and usually a qualifier for handicap purposes. It attracts the better players and potential new members who are serious about their golf, for it offers four more qualifying rounds a month on top of the monthly medal. 'Our handicaps are on the line throughout the year, come rain or shine,' said Ren. 'You and me Chris, Ian, John and Norman, we have realistic handicaps.' 'Yes, you're right Ren, for just as our handicap comes down after a good round, it goes up point one every time we have a bad one,' I replied. 'It's all very well to say you have been a single figure man for the last thirty years, when you don't bother to enter competitions any more. I wonder what some of their handicaps would be if they competed as regularly as we do?' I said. 'Not single figures I'll warrant,' said Ren, with a knowing smile.

There is a nucleus of about twenty members who play in the competition on Tuesdays throughout the year, which swells to forty or more when the chaps who work can join in on a summer's evening. It only costs £2 to enter and the club keeps nothing back; so all the entry money goes towards prizes to be spent at the pro's shop and of course the club bar benefits. You can only play in two or three balls, so if all five of us who regularly play together turn up, we split up. We usually play as late as possible, because Renald Jupp (always known as Ren) although my age, still has his own business. Ian Kenyon is Head of Geology at nearby Truro school, John Wills is an osteopath (he has offered us half price manipulations, but none of us have yet dared take up his offer!) and Norman Kirton is head of the Customs & Excise department in Truro. We have devised an interesting way to have a wager on the game. We play for £2, the same as the entry fee; the best card takes the money from the other two and buys the first round of drinks, the worst card buys the second round of drinks and the man in the middle buys the peanuts or cashew nuts. One tie, all tie and no money changes hands. 'Looks as though you and I are playing for the peanuts today, Chris,' said Ian, when Ren was running away with it. 'I've just remembered a very pressing appointment lads, I must go straight after the game,' I said – I was ten shots behind and looking a certainty for the second round of drinks. 'You can pay up first or you'll be going to your appointment on flat tyres,' was the response.

Often it all comes down to the last putt on the last green to establish the winner and you can imagine the leg pulling then. Good golf in good company, is what it's all about.

Long stockings to just below the knees when wearing shorts, has always been considered sartorially correct, wherever I have played overseas in the past – a little nicety which seems to have sadly fallen away. I asked the secretary at Royal Port Alfred last year, 'Why is it that nobody wears long stockings on the course anymore. I always remember your club being so correct in observing such formalities?' 'I know,' he replied ruefully. 'Our wealthy country members who come down each holiday from Joburg to their palatial, seaside houses won't wear long stockings anymore,' he went on, obviously unhappy about it. 'But we need their business and they say it's no longer 'de rigueur' on the Joburg courses, so we have had to reluctantly follow suit,' he said. The same seems to have happened everywhere else both in South Africa and here in England – a general lowering of standards I call it – but of course I am now looked upon as an old fuddy-duddy in any case. As far as I am concerned I shall continue to wear long stockings on the golf course when I am wearing shorts – fuddy-duddy or not – I don't feel properly dressed without them.

We had just finished putting on the 2nd green one day and were walking towards the next tee, when Paul Matthews from the four behind us – looking somewhat unusually agitated for him – said, 'Chris, you didn't see a ball over the mounds on the 2nd did you? I've just hit the biggest drive I've ever hit on that hole, straight down the middle of the fairway and we couldn't find it,' he said. I looked crestfallen, I had picked up the ball – I had assumed it had fallen out of someone's bag – for I thought that no one could possibly drive that far. 'I'm terribly sorry Paul,' I said, 'here it is,' and I fished it out of my bag and handed it to him, very shamefaced. It's since become a locker room joke at Perranporth and in the nicest possible way, he will never allow me to forget it. Paul is a tall 6'4" Cornishman with a lovely easy sense of humour, a good golfer and very popular with the other members. He knows I love a joke and usually has one ready for me when we meet at the club. One in particular, he told me last year, has become my party piece when in mixed company.

A fellow was walking his dog in Boscawen Park, Truro, when he saw an old man sitting on a park bench, sobbing his heart out. He went up to him and enquired, 'What's the matter Sir, it's very upsetting seeing an old gentleman like you so obviously unhappy?' The tears were still rolling down the old man's face as he said, 'I got married three weeks ago to the most lovely young girl of 35, she has already proved the most wonderful wife,' and the old man took out his handkerchief and tried to staunch the tears running freely down his cheeks. Then he went on, 'We would wake up early in the morning and make love before breakfast, then she would go off to work and I would have a meal ready for her when she came back at lunchtime. After lunch we would make love again. When she got back from work at half past five, she would immediately set to and make a mouth watering three course dinner, which we would eat together and then we would make love again as soon as we were in bed.' The tears continued to roll down the old man's cheeks. 'Well sir, with a lovely young wife like you've just described, how can you be so unhappy?' asked the man with the dog. 'Because,' the old man sobbed, 'I can't remember where I live!'

Gary Marson asked if he could join Ian, Ren and me one Tuesday –it was before the club banned play in fourballs. 'Of course,' I said and we decided it would be easier to start at the 10th that day.

Gary is a robust fellow in his late forties, with a round, rose red cherubic like face and a quiff of straw coloured hair standing straight up above his forehead. Either he or Gerald Gunn, one or the other, can usually be found playing the fruit machine in the bar, when not on the golf course. Gary has a most unorthodox but very effective swing and plays off five or six handicap. I know he's not the only one, but he has a very bad habit of walking ahead of his playing partners, once he has played his shot. We were only on our second hole that day – the 11th, a par five – and I had a four wood to the green for my third shot, when I shouted to him, 'Just move over a bit Gary in case I knobble it.' 'Right,' he called back, but only moved about three yards. I still wasn't too happy, but he could see me as he was standing on an elevated mound. So I played the shot, it went low and hard out of the heel of the club, which, according to Ren and Ian would have made the green 160 yards away, if it hadn't hit Gary full in the chest and knocked him backwards. He was mesmerised by the shot – like a rabbit awaiting death by a stoat or a weasel – he seemed transfixed to the spot and unable to move out of the balls way. By the grace of God it hit him on the right side of his chest, if it had hit him on the left side, it could have killed him. I was so shaken I proceeded to take a nine, it was the first time I had ever hit anybody with a golf ball. 'I'm OK, I'll finish the round,' he said when he had picked himself up and to his great credit he did. His chest was still black and blue a few days later and of all things he said it had caused him to start shanking, but very fortunately he had no lasting ill effects.

'The two old fools who will play in any weather,' is how Ren and I have been branded. In the early days before John and Norman joined us, and with Ian teaching, there were sometimes only three or four people in the Tuesday competition when the weather was bad, two of whom were always Ren and me. I remember one competition in early March particularly. It was blowing a howling gale from the north west and literally belting down with rain. We were on the 12th. I looked across at Ren and my eyes pleaded with him; let's call it a day. He just smiled and we carried on and he won the competition as usual, for he is an excellent bad weather golfer.

Ren was also very well placed to win one day when playing with myself and Bob Gillman. It had been building up for a storm for sometime, but as we had never had a nil return together we kept going, rather than walk in. Suddenly, half way up the 15th, there was a flash of lightning from immediately above, followed instantly by a great roll of thunder and the strong smell of cordite all around us. We needed no further warning, we grabbed our golf balls and ran for the clubhouse and safety. I've never been closer to being struck by lightning and it wasn't a pleasant experience.

'Can I come through?' said the well-spoken gentleman as we left the 10th green. 'No,' said Ren peremptorily. 'But I'm the Captain of Toffee Nose Country Club in Surrey,' he continued. 'I don't care if you are the Captain of the R&A, a golfer on his own has no standing, you can't come through,' replied Ren, getting more and more agitated. Ian and I drove at the 11th and then Ren duffed his tee shot into the gorse in front (I've never seen him do it before) and eventually got out onto the fairway for six, watched all the time by the visiting captain with a supercilious smile on his face. Infuriatingly he was quite obviously a very good golfer and he was on our tail throughout the nine, but we didn't let him come through. Perhaps fortunately the 'visiting captain' disappeared after the round, for Ian and I were quite sure that a major confrontation was brewing up between Ren and him, for Ren was still simmering with rage an hour after.

Rather curiously Ian always marks his ball with a green arrow (whether he was a convict in a previous life or whether he has aspirations to being one, I have never asked him), but during one round together he lost his ball in the thick rough to the left of the 7th fairway. It was a medal that day, so Ian walked back and played three off the tee and from then on we were being pushed from behind by a fellow playing on his own. Ian lost his ball again on the 13th and whilst we were looking for it the fellow behind had the audacity to drive through us. Just as he drew level with us, I found Ian's ball and shouted, 'Here it is Ian, green arrow as usual isn't it?' The chap rather surprisingly said to us, 'No, that's my ball,' walked over and picked it up and proceeded to the 14th tee and drove off. We were so utterly flabbergasted by this, that neither of us said anything and then at the same time we found Ian's other ball also with a green arrow on it. So this gentleman had presumably found Ian's lost ball in the rough at the 7th, decided to play with it and had had the gall to call himself through. We had a good laugh then and it hasn't lost any mileage since in the re-telling.

On the northern edge of the course next to the 12th and 13th holes is a very large holiday caravan park, which at the height of the season in August is full to capacity with visitors. They seem to think that despite the signs warning them of the dangers, it is their absolute right to fly kites or model aeroplanes, or just to wander across the course, instead of around it, on their way to and from the beach. As the 13th is a partially blind tee shot, there is also a big danger that an unsuspecting person may be struck by a stray ball. For the major competitions in July and August we have a ranger in a buggy – usually Fred Roberts – who has the task of warning people of the danger they are in, in a diplomatic way, so as not to get their backs up. I was one of the first off with Chris Jeffrey, in Perranporth's main 36 hole competition of the year, the 'Perran Sands' Trophy. We had driven at the 13th – before Fred arrived in his buggy to give us the all clear – and as we crested the rise halfway up the fairway, we saw a little boy who had a ball in his hand and was heading hot foot for the nearest caravan. 'Oi!' roared Chris (he was an ex-regular in the military police and had a stentorian voice to match), 'bring that ball back here!' and advanced threateningly towards the boy. At the same moment I noticed an enormous shirtless man, head shaved and chest and arms covered in tattoos, standing in the doorway of the caravan. Hello I thought to myself, here we go, big trouble; but the little boy turned round and brought the ball back to us and the brute in the doorway of the caravan, presumably the boy's father, waved and his face broke into a broad smile – confrontation over – phew!

Norman Kirton told me that he was in the same fourball as Phil Wilkes, who was playing particularly badly that day, when he hit a high shank with a driver off the 13th tee and the ball shot off at right angles. It not only hit a caravan, but went straight through an open roof fanlight and landed on a table next to a little boy reading a comic. The whole family came running out of the caravan and a good deal of explanation was necessary on Norman and Phil's part, to explain away such a fluke. I was having a similarly bad time one day when I drove off the 14th tee and the ball came off the toe of the driver straight towards cover point and landed on the corrugated iron roof of a nearby shelter, with a very loud bang. It was in a bad lie near the shelter when I got there and my next duff shot, as luck would have it, went full toss and irrecoverable, straight down a rabbit hole. 'Bad luck,' and broad grins, was all the sympathy I got from Ren and Ian.

In 1995 I played in the 'Perran Sands' with Peter Bayly and John Archer; it turned out to be one of the most amusing day's golf I can remember and I have recounted the incidents that happened that day many times. Peter Bayly a Londoner is 56 and ten years younger than me and it wasn't long after my arrival at Perranporth that we were playing regularly together. He is an architect and has a practice in Truro, but when he moved house south of Truro near the river, he decided that Truro Golf Club would be more convenient for him, so he left Perranporth and I for one sorely miss his company. John Archer is now President of the club. Perhaps around 50, he is slim and of medium height, prematurely grey and always has a happy smile on his face and an infectious chuckle, so that even the dourest member is soon laughing with him. He could hit the ball a country mile, but because of a very strong grip, he was never quite sure in which direction the ball was likely to go. He has since modified his grip and become a better golfer – but in those days his left hand was so far over and right hand so far under the shaft – that there was little wonder he had problems with control and direction, it was thus rare indeed that his ball visited the fairway.

July 28th 1995 was a hot sultry day with little wind and it soon became apparent, that the continual criss-crossing of the fairways to help John find his ball in the rough, was exhausting us, particularly Peter. After a couple of holes in the second round, following the indiscretion of a hearty lunch, Peter said to me, 'Chris, I can't take any more of this, you help John find his ball from now on,' and he proceeded to plod straight down the middle of each fairway, eyes glazed with fatigue, with the one thought only of finishing the round. John meanwhile had a fourteen at the par five, 5th. He went from one side of the course to the other, losing his ball four times in the process and arrived to the right of the green for eight (by which time Peter was beginning to look totally shattered). Fortunately I watched his next shot, he hadn't a clue himself where it had gone, which was a shank over the 6th tee into deep rough and was accompanied by an infectious giggle. He then had an almighty hack with a wedge and succeeded in getting the ball out just clear of the rough – ten! Then followed a cameo of sheer perfection with an exquisite chip onto the green. And three putts for a fourteen. Vintage Archer!

Chapter Twelve
Aussie

Would you like to hear about my round?'

I just love to watch people's reactions, when you ask them that question. Our chief bar steward at Perranporth golf club, Ian McKechnie, has perfected his response to the question – no doubt after much practise in front of his mirror – his eye's go completely blank and he looks straight through you. Then he will say something like, 'Can I first serve these six people here and then perhaps ... no ... I'll tell you what, let's add it to the other fifteen rounds you're going to tell me about Chris, I really can't wait,' and a broad smile will light up his face.

The late much lamented Eddie Arthur, was generally acknowledged as the authority on ball-by-ball accounts. Eddie was a short thick set man with a shock of white hair, strong hands and powerful shoulders – all from a lifetime of hard manual work – and he had the reputation of being able to remember just about every round he had ever played. He was never happier than when telling you about them, in his attractive Cornish burr. He used to be a fixture at the bar after the Sunday morning round, regaling all and sundry who were prepared to listen. He always had a liquid lunch on Sunday and by the time his wife arrived to drive him home, much the worse for wear, he would have a happy contented smile on his broad weather beaten face.

Ian McKechnie is a good friend of Eddie's son and one of his favourite stories is about Eddie returning home following a round at Perran, just as he and Eddie's son were about to go out. 'Had a great round today son, my second shot to the 1st was hit a bit thin, but ...' started Eddie. 'Hang on a minute father,' said his son interrupting him, 'Ian and I are just finishing our tea and then we're going out to the pub together, start at the 15th father, will you?' Without breaking stride, Eddie immediately started again at the 15th and took them through, blow by blow, to the 18th green. I never tire of hearing that one and from the animated expression on his face, Ian equally enjoys telling it.

I had a piece of good fortune twelve months after our return to England. I landed a summer evening's only job from March to October each year. Myself and my part-time employees call on people throughout Cornwall and ask them to consider becoming members of a well-known charity. It is interesting and rewarding work and it also allows me to play my golf when I want to and we are then free to go on holiday in November for a couple of months and miss the worst of the English winter.

I certainly never expected to be able to visit South Africa the five times that we have done, interspersed with a holiday one year in Australia and another year in Malta. Dare I say that perhaps my good fortune was to a certain extent deserved, for in hindsight I had the guts to leave South Africa when I did and deep down feel the country owes me something because of the indecent haste with which it was handed over to majority rule. Perhaps I was a little naïve, but when I arrived from Rhodesia in 1978, I fully expected to spend the rest of my life, in a stable and responsible white ruled South Africa.

We stay each year at the hot and humid Natal South Coast, on the outskirts of Margate and ironically only fifteen miles south of Port Shepstone, where I used to live and work, over twenty years ago. Gill's sister owns a cottage in a large secure retirement village – which used to be their late mother's – and we lease it from Ann, who lives in Johannesburg. We are now overseas members of Margate Country Club only five minutes drive away. The members love to say to me with a smug look on their faces, 'Out here again to take advantage of our week rand eh, like Mike Downs and Bob Wright I suppose?' 'Yes, we're out again, but unlike Mike and Bob we used to live here, we were South Africans like you are.' Downs and Wright are both retired Englishmen, who went out on holiday to South Africa and quickly realised it is far cheaper to live there for half the year, than in England, with the glorious warm weather as an added bonus. They don't concern themselves with the politics of the country and if and when the shit hits the fan, they can just return to their homes in England and look for somewhere else. 'We'll play, two, two, four, two – pounds if we win, rands if we lose,' the locals will say when playing against me, digging each other in the ribs and falling about laughing – they love their bit of fun.

The one big drawback of playing golf in high summer where we stay is the humidity and oppressive heat, which hits you harder each year, as you get older. I use sun cream and take plenty of water onto the course with me, to ward off dehydration and I'm not afraid to use an umbrella as a parasol – far better to be thought effeminate – than to get sunstroke. I play in a competition every Thursday and Saturday at Margate and sometimes in a mixed competition on Sundays with Gill and much to the amusement of the macho South African men, I caddy for my wife on Tuesday mornings in the ladies only competitions.

Other than Margate there is a very good course at Southbroom a little further down the coast and of course my old club when I lived in the area, Port Shepstone.

Shortly after we arrive from the UK in mid November, there is the annual 'Rhodesians Worldwide' Golf Competition for ex-Rhodesians held each year at Umkomaas, thirty miles south of Durban. It's very well run and always fully subscribed each year and the proceeds go to help those Rhodesians/Zimbabweans who have fallen upon hard times. The organisers give of their time freely and do a sterling job; it's known as the 'Rhodesian spirit' and it will never die, whatever the adversity.

I was putting on the 1st green at Margate four years ago, when suddenly I got the dreaded 'yips' – I couldn't get the putter back, never mind bring it forward again. I struggled with it and tried everything – I even putted for a year with my driver – until when playing with Gary Faraway one day at Perranporth, he said to me, 'Why don't you try putting cack-handed Chris, left hand below right?' 'OK,' I replied. 'I'll try anything,' for I was becoming desperate. It worked, but now I only use it for the short putts under eight feet.

I still hold the record of a six on the short par four thirteenth at Perran – with five drivers and a wedge – in fact it was a good drive, a wedge onto the green and four putts with the driver!

Early in the nineteen nineties we tried a five week holiday in December/January in Malta. It wasn't a success; the island is desperately overcrowded and consequently has only one golf course which we played once, not memorably, because it was very wet on the day we played and very expensive. Malta seems to cater mainly for Germans and other eastern European countries in high summer and our presence in the off-season seemed to be resented by the hotel staff and we were consequently treated like second-class citizens. The dining room of the hotel was more like a works canteen and a line of scruffy looking specimens plonked the food on our plates looking totally disinterested. It reminded me of National Service basic training in the army, where we were similarly treated in the cookhouse, by surly, often dirty army cooks. Our bedroom for the first week of the stay was immediately above reception and we soon realised what a disadvantage that was. People called at reception at all hours of the day and night, finally culminating in a drunken Scotsman staggering in there, in the early hours of New Year's Day, bawling his head off. We changed rooms the following morning. Malta is also virtually bereft of birds; we only ever saw house sparrows and feral pigeons, any other birds large or small, were presumably shot on sight, for the island is ringed by shooting butts. We won't be going on holiday there again in a hurry.

'Gooday mate,' the young man said as I collected my morning newspaper. 'What did you say?' I asked him. 'I said gooday mate,' he replied. If there is one thing I hate more than anything else, it is being called mate. You can call me – old boy, old man, old chap, old fellow, old fart even, or call me by my surname only – but please not mate.

Gill and I went on a five-week holiday to Queensland, Australia in November/December 1996. We were forewarned that its is the hottest time of the year there, but at any other time I am still working, so we had no alternative if we wanted to see the country. It was on the Sunshine Coast north of Brisbane, where early each morning I met the seventeen year old youth who referred to me as mate and of course I had to get used to it, for I told myself that he doesn't know any better and it was his country I was visiting after all.

We joined Mount Coolum Golf Club for the period of our stay there, situated appropriately next to an enormous round-topped mountain of that name. The course had a lot of trees on it – principally gum – and many water hazards and on three sides thick impenetrable bush. 'Don't go in there mate, there are deadly poisonous snakes in there mate,' they said. But I wasn't going to abandon my ball each time it went into the bush, so I went in there and usually found it and often other balls as well, but I never saw a snake. This reaction to snakes surprised me, for I had always thought of the Aussies as tough outdoor types and sometimes when it was really hot – burning heat, hotter than I have ever experienced before – many of the locals themselves wouldn't play. The only way I could face the heat was to put a wet towel under my floppy hat to protect my thinning pate and even then the sun burned through remorselessly. I was playing off nine at the time and found to my astonishment that there were only a couple of golfers with lower handicaps than mine in the club. For the first time I encountered men with handicaps up to 36 and women as high as 45 handicap. When a chap playing off 25 won the monthly medal and the handsome sum of $60, with a quite ludicrous score of net 65, I went up to the Captain and said, 'How many shots are you going to cut him, at least six I'll warrant?' 'No, I don't think I'll cut him this time, it's his first win,' the Captain replied. I was flabbergasted. 'You're joking surely,' I said. 'No, I'm not. That's the way we do things here and I'm not going to change it,' answered the Captain, and that was that. Gill reminded me that lady beginners in England start off with a 45 handicap, but 28 is the highest I have known a man to be given, even a rank beginner. So my preconceived image of the tough macho male Aussie striving to emulate their heroes, like fellow Aussie Greg Norman, was quickly shattered – many of them are just ringers!

'Don't bother about the line Chris mate – just putt out,' they said. The monthly medals are played in fourballs – a first for me – the greens were so perfect that it wasn't necessary to mark your ball, you just putted out and it had the added advantage of speeding up the game.

'What on earth is that funny little fellow?' I asked. 'That's a willie wagtail mate – they are very friendly little birds,' said my Aussie playing partner and with that he took some pieces of bread out of a packet he had brought with him and the bird came and ate it out of his hand. The willie wagtail spreads out its tail like a fan and then gyrates it from side to side (which is how it got it's name) and at the same time makes funny chirping noises. It was a most amusing sight. There were flocks of cockatoos everywhere; wonderful different shades of white and pink with crests that rise and fall as they landed and took off and we were awakened just before first light each morning by the insane cackling of the kookaburra – a very large member of the kingfisher family – known also not surprisingly, as the 'laughing jackass.'

I saw my first wild pelicans – enormous birds with equally enormous bills – feeding on the mudflats beside a river and a koala bear absolutely motionless, clinging to a tree looking very sleepy and disinterested. We were told where we could find kangaroos. A whole family of them were grazing open grassland, which was interspersed with huge clumps of gum trees. I found it strangely moving to be so close to such wonderful animals and I wondered what the transported felons from the old country thought, when they first encountered these strange creatures.

Throughout our stay in Australia we saw not even one Aborigine, during the entire five weeks. Could it be – that compared to South Africa and the rest of what was once colonial Africa – the Australians have somehow got it right? I am told that there are 2 million aborigines in the country to approximately 16 million whites. Despite the heat and the forthright brashness of the average Aussie, the country must be one of the most sought after destinations in the world to emigrate to. I certainly missed a golden opportunity when I turned down the offer of a £10 passage in 1963.

It has often struck me as strange that when I dream about playing golf – which is often – it hasn't been about winning 'The Open' or winning the club championship. Surprisingly I dream about being late on the tee, or being left behind by the other three members of my fourball whilst trying to find my ball or, the most bizarre of all, there not being sufficient room on the tee to play my shot. When I try to analyse this last predicament; there is always a tree or a bush in the way, or I can't complete my backswing because people watching are crowding me in and then when I finally make contact, I hit it only about ten yards or keep having air shots – my dreams are always the same. Yet when I am back on the rugby field, I'm playing for Bideford, I'm over sixty and I've been persuaded to come out of retirement and I always play a blinder. This dream contrast of mine is very odd.

I have as many as five 'top of the range' woods and I use the latest 'fly further' golf ball; so it is not too difficult to keep to 10 or 11 handicap and I still cling to the forlorn hope of single figures again. Thirty five years ago when my father was the same age as I am now, the equipment available for him to play with was infinitely inferior and the fact that he maintained a 12 handicap then, was an achievement in itself.

For the last eighteen years I have kept my own 'golf results' book – who I played with, my score, handicap change and the eclectic for the year on my home course – it's proved very useful to refer back to and to settle disputes. Eating healthily, watching my weight, a two mile brisk walk before breakfast every weekday morning, ten minutes exercises twice a week before the morning walk and above all else no booze on Mondays and Fridays have kept me remarkably fit over the years – I have missed very little golf. I have also always pulled my own trolley and will endeavour to continue doing so as long as possible.

At the risk of being accused of plagiarism, I look forward to the start of my forty eighth year of playing golf with these thoughts – Oh more than happy 'golfer', if he doth but know his good fortune!